FOOD OF THE PHILIPPINES
Published by PERIPLUS EDITIONS
(HK) LTD.,
with editorial offices at
153 Milk Street, Boston MA 02109
and 5 Little Road #08-01
Singapore 536983.

Copyright © 1998
Periplus Editions (HK) Ltd.

Hardcover ISBN: 962-593-245-3

LCC Number 98-87580

Publisher: Eric Oey
Editors: Melanie Raymond and
Elizabeth V. Reyes
Production: Violet Wong
PRINTED IN SINGAPORE.

Distributed by

USA
Charles E. Tuttle Co., Inc.
RRI Box 231-5
North Clarendon, VT 05759-9700
Toll Free Tel.: (800) 526-2778
Tel.: (802) 773-8930
Fax.: (802) 773-6993

Japan
Tuttle Shokai, Inc.
21–13, Seki, Tamu-ku,
Kawasaki-shi
Kanagawa-ken 214-0022, Japan
Tel.: (813) 3811-7741
Fax.: (813) 5689-4926

Asia-Pacific
Berkeley Books Pte. Ltd
5 Little Road, #08-01
Singapore 536983
Tel.: (65) 280-3320
Fax.: (65) 280-6290

Credits
All food photographs by Luca Invernizzi Tettoni. Additional photos by: Photobank Sing., pages 2, 6, 14, 17; Jill Gocher, pages 11, 21; Sonny Yabao, pages 7, 8, 10, 12, 13, 15, 16, 18, 20. Photograph of author by Mindy Gana. Fiesta print on page 9 reproduced courtesy of the Gallery of Prints in Manila.

First edition
1 3 5 7 9 10 8 6 4 2
05 04 03 02 01 00 99 98

THE FOOD OF THE
PHILIPPINES

Authentic Recipes from the Pearl of the Orient

Text and recipes by Reynaldo G. Alejandro
Introductory articles by Doreen G. Fernandez,
Corazon S. Alvina and Millie Reyes
Food photography by Luca Invernizzi Tettoni

Featuring recipes from the following restaurants
Cafe Ysabel
Hidden Valley Springs Resort
The Manila Hotel
Skyline Restaurant
Villa Escudero Plantations and Resort
The Westin Philippine Plaza

PERIPLUS

Contents

Part One: Food in the Philippines

Islands with a history of colonization
nourished a people with a gift for adaptation

By Doreen Fernandez

What is Filipino food? Is it *adobo*—which has a Spanish name, yet covers chicken, pork, vegetables or even seafood stewed in vinegar and garlic, and is thus unlike any Spanish *adobado*? Or is it *pansit*—noodles of many persuasions, found on many tables and utilizing local ingredients, yet obviously of Chinese origin? Or would it be *sinigang*—the sour broth allied to similar Southeast Asian soup-stews—that's cooling in hot tropical weather? Could it even be the omnipresent fried chicken—sometimes marinated in vinegar and garlic before it is fried? Or *arroz caldo*—a chicken congee that is popular even on airlines as comfort food? Could it be all of the above? Where did it all begin, where did it come from and how did it develop?

The land and the waters gave the Filipinos their food. Seven thousand and more islands are surrounded by seas, threaded by rivers and brooks, edged by swamps and dotted with lakes, canals, ponds and lagoons, providing a multitude of fish and other water creatures that comprise the basic food of Filipinos. This variegated land of mountains and plains, shores and forests, fields and hills is inhabited by land and air creatures that generously transform into food. It also brings forth greenery all year-round, a garden of edible grains, leaves, roots, fruits, pods, seeds, tendrils and flowers.

Thus, the Filipino diet pattern: rice as a staple, steamed white and plain, providing background to the flavors of fish, meat and vegetables. It is, nutritionists judge, one of the healthiest eating patterns in the world.

Because the island geography makes food easily accessible to hunters, fishermen, food gatherers and farmers, indigenous food is simply cooked: grilled (*inihaw*), steamed (*pinasingawan*) or boiled (*nilaga*). Or it may be untouched by fire, as is *kinilaw*, fish briefly marinated in vinegar or lime juice to transform it from rawness, while retaining freshness and translucence.

Since food is one of the liveliest areas of popular culture, it has of course been friendly to foreign influences, and to change. Chinese traders, the Spanish, colonizers and proselytizers both, and in the 20th century, the United States—all left their mark on the local food. The signature ingredients of the Southeast Asian neighbors are present too, in the form of chilies, lemongrass and fragrant/pungent fishsauce, called *patis*. Recent times have seen foods from other more distant lands sometimes occuping a small corner of the Filipino table.

To the question therefore, What is Filipino food? One can answer, all of the above.

Page 2:
Emerald green rice terraces are part of the spectacular scenery in the Cordillera of Northern Philippines.
Opposite:
Stuffed Crab (recipe page 64) and Boiled Shrimp. The Filipinos took to the Spanish technique of rellenado *or "stuffing" with relish.*

What is Filipino Food?

Indigenous dishes blended with flavors brought by Chinese traders and the spices of the conquistadores comprise this versatile cuisine.

By Doreen Fernandez

The Philippines country culture starts in a tropical clime divided into rainy and dry seasons and an archipelago with 7,000 islands. These isles contain the Cordillera mountains, Luzon's central plains, Palawan's coral reefs; seas touching the world's longest discontinuous coastline; and a multitude of lakes, rivers, springs and brooks.

The population—120 different ethnic groups and the mainstream communities of Tagalog/Ilocano/Pampango/Pangasinan and Visayan lowlanders—worked within a gentle but lush environment. In it they shaped their own lifeways: building houses, weaving cloth, telling and writing stories; ornamenting and decorating, preparing food.

Foreign influences made deep impact on native island culture. The Chinese traders, who had been coming to the islands since the 11th century, brought silks and ceramics, took away products from the forest and sea, and left behind them many traditions so deeply embedded in daily life that Filipinos do not realize their provenance. Filipinos of Chinese ancestry comprise an important facet of the national profile.

In the 16th century, the Spanish colonizers imported Christianity, and the culture related to a colonization that lasted three centuries. Families were "brought within the sound of church bells"; and thus were created villages, towns and cities. Spanish cultural forms replaced or melded with indigenous expressions. The folk cultures of the Christianized lowlands are thus greatly Hispanicized, as against the Cordillera highlands (later reached by Protestant missionaries) and Mindanao (where the Muslims long resisted Spanish colonization).

After the Revolution of 1889, the Battle of Manila Bay, and the pact of exchange between the US and Spain, the country became an American colony. The US-style government and educational system imported along with the popular culture made Filipinos the most "Americanized Asians", and the Philippines one of the larger English-speaking countries of the world.

Left:
Bringing in what has to be the catch of the day, General Santos City, Mindanao.
Opposite:
Nature's plenty: a feast of rice, fish, fruit and vegetables.

Fresh food market in Tagaytay, a temperate city located high above Taal Lake in Southern Luzon. Tagaytay is well known for its market gardens and fruit stalls.

When restaurants were established in the 19th century, Chinese food became a staple of the *pansiterias*, with the food given Spanish names for the ease of the clientele: thus *comida China* (Chinese food) includes *arroz caldo* (rice and chicken gruel); and *morisqueta tostada* (fried rice).

When the Spaniards came, the food influences they brought were from both Spain and Mexico, as it was through the vice-royalty of Mexico that the Philippines were governed.

This storied history and Mother Nature's largesse combined and evolved to produce Filipino food.

The Chinese who came to trade sometimes stayed on. Their foodways accompanied them and also stayed. Perhaps they cooked the noodles of home; certainly they used local condiments; surely they taught their Filipino wives their dishes, and thus Filipino-Chinese food came to be. The names identify them: *pansit* (Hokkien for something quickly cooked) are noodles; *lumpia* are vegetables rolled in edible wrappers; *siopao* are steamed, filled buns; *siomai* are dumplings.

All, of course, came to be indigenized—Filipinized by the ingredients and by local tastes. Today, for example, *Pansit Malabon* has oysters and squid, since Malabon is a fishing center; and *Pansit Marilao* is sprinkled with rice crisps, because the town is within the Luzon rice bowl.

This meant the production of food for an elite, non-food-producing class, and a food for which many ingredients were not locally available.

Fil-Hispanic food had new flavors and ingredients–olive oil, paprika, saffron, ham, cheese, cured sausages—and new names. *Paella*, the dish cooked in the fields by Spanish workers, came to be a festive dish combining pork, chicken, seafood, ham, sausages and vegetables, a luxurious mix of the local and the foreign. *Relleno*, the process of stuffing festive capons and turkeys for Christmas, was applied to chickens, and even to *bangus*, the silvery milkfish. Christmas, a new feast for Filipinos that coincided with the rice harvest, came to feature not only the myriad native rice cakes, but also *ensaymadas* (brioche-like cakes buttered, sugared and cheese-sprinkled) to dip in hot thick chocolate, and the apples, oranges, chestnuts and walnuts of European

Christmases. Even the Mexican corn *tamal* turned Filipino, becoming rice-based *tamales* wrapped in banana leaves.

The Americans introduced to Philippine cuisine the ways of convenience: pressure-cooking, freezing, pre-cooking; sandwiches and salads; hamburgers, fried chicken and steaks.

Add to the above other cuisines found in the country along with other global influences: French, Italian, Middle Eastern, Japanese, Thai, Vietnamese. They grow familiar, but remain "imported" and not yet indigenized.

On a buffet table today one might find, for example, *kinilaw na tanguingue*, mackerel dressed with vinegar, ginger, onions, hot peppers, perhaps coconut milk; also grilled tiger shrimp, and maybe *sinigang na baboy*, pork and vegetables in a broth soured with tamarind, all from the native repertoire. Alongside there would almost certainly be *pansit*, noodles once Chinese, now Filipino, still in a sweet-sour sauce. Spanish festive fare like *morcon* (beef rolls), *embutido* (pork rolls), fish *escabeche* and stuffed chicken or turkey might be there too. The centerpiece would probably be *lechon*, spit-roasted pig, which may be Chinese or Polynesian in influence, but bears a Spanish name, and may therefore derive from *cochinillo asado*. Vegetable dishes could include an American salad and a *pinakbet* (vegetables and shrimp paste). The dessert table would

'Fête à Santa-Cruz de Nano", (1887) by Marcelle Lancelot (after Andrews). First published in LuCon et Palaouan: Six Années de Voyage aux Philippines by Alfred Marché. This engraving depicts Manileno ilustrados enjoying a neighborhood party. Ilustrados, meaning "enlightened ones", comprised an elite urban class with a high level of education and nationalism.

surely be richly Spanish: *leche flan* (caramel custard), *natilla, yemas, dulces de naranja, membrillo, torta del rey*, etc., but also include local fruits in syrup (coconut, santol, guavas) and American cakes and pies. The global village may be reflected in *shawarma* and pasta. The buffet table and Filipino food today is thus a gastronomic telling of Philippine history.

What really is Philippine food, then? Indigenous food from land and sea, field and forest. Also and of course: dishes and culinary procedures from China, Spain, Mexico, and the United States, and more recently from further abroad.

What makes them Philippine? The history and society that introduced and adapted them; the people who tuned them to their tastes and accepted them into their homes and restaurants, and especially the harmonizing culture that combined them into contemporary Filipino fare.

Regional Dishes

In this land of more than 7,000 islands, regional diversity can not only be seen but tasted.

By Corazon S. Alvina

The Philippine archipelago has conjured a people with a stubborn sense of regional identity. The scattered island geography sustains multiple cultures—and many distinctly different cuisines, all alive and well. Regionalism can be sensed—ay, tasted—on Philippine islanders' taste buds.

While Filipino food comprises essentially a simple, tropical cuisine, diverse styles have evolved among seven major regions of the 7,107 islands. The variations are traceable to the character of, first, the natural resources—the produce of different soils and seas, plants and animals, and to the regional character of different island peoples—separate, insular, fractionalized (and proud of their differences). The basic foodstuffs and condiments become more interesting when explored among insular places.

The northwest coast of Luzon is the Ilocos region, a strip of land between the mountains and the sea, where five provinces share the same language, food and tough challenges of nature. Ilocanos are frugal and hardy, relying on what can be coaxed from the dry, hot land. They eat meat sparingly, preferring vegetables and rice as the bulk of their diet.

Pinakbet is a popular vegetable medley identified with the Ilocanos, a combination of tomatoes, eggplant and bitter melon, lima beans, okra, and squash—all bound together with *bagoong*, a salty sauce made from fermented fish or shrimp.

Ilocanos' meat dishes lean toward high cholesterol: *lomo*, a pork liver and kidneys soup; *longganisa*, a fatty ground-pork sausage enjoyed for breakfast; and *bagnet*, dried pork belly, deep fried with *bagoong*.

Two cuisines in the rice-and-sugar lands of Central Luzon—Pampanga and Bulacan—claim superiority over the other. In Pampanga food is a major preoccupation; the cuisine is ornate and lavish, like their wood carving. Many exotic dishes are attributed to land-locked Pampanga: fried catfish with *buro*, a fermented rice sauce; fermented crabs; frogs or milkfish in a sour soup; fried mole crickets, and cured pork slices called *tosino*.

As a sugar-producing province, Pampanga sweet-

Tribal women from Cotobato in Southern Mindanao. Much of the rice, corn and coconuts eaten throughout the Philippines is grown in the rich agricultural island of Mindanao.

ens many of her dishes—especially desserts! There are Spanish-influenced cream puffs, egg yolk custards, *turrones*, marzipans and meringues; plus the very native *tibok-tibok* (water buffalo milk blended with corn). From here comes *bringhe* (a fiesta rice made with coconut milk); *ensaymada*, a buttery bun; *leche flan*, a crème brûlée made with water buffalo milk; and a great array of sticky rice cakes.

In Bulacan, the motto is not to eat anything unless it makes you swoon with pleasure. Bulacan cooking is unhurried, old-fashioned, sure, and very varied, based on wide ingredient resources. River fish are boiled with citrus or in palm wine, then flamed. Eels are simmered in coconut cream; saltwater fish, in vinegar and ginger. Mudfish are fermented or packed in banana stalks and buried in live coals; crabs sautéed with guava; shellfish flavored in a gingery broth. Bulakeños specialize in meat dishes: A chicken "sits" in a claypot lined with salt and is slowly roasted. Typically, Bulakan cooks claim the best *relleno* and *galantina* (stuffed chicken rolls); *estofado* (pork leg) and *asado* (pot roast); and *kare-kare* (oxtail stewed in peanut sauce).

Homes around Manila Bay harbor Filipinos' favorite comfort-foods, conjured from ingredients derived from around the metropolis. Fresh seafood comes in by the fishing port to the north; meats and fowl are trucked in from the south; vegetables and rice are grown on the plains of Central Luzon.

Several dishes comprise the "national" cuisine: *bistek* (beef and onion rings braised in soy sauce); *lumpia* (spring rolls); and the popular *adobo*— chicken and pork stewed in vinegar and soy sauce, garlic, peppercorns and bay leaf. Every province

Seafood is an important part of the diet in most of the Philippines, as you would expect in an archipelagic nation.

boasts of having the best version of *adobo*. Manila's is soupy with soy sauce and garlic. Cavite cooks mash pork liver into the sauce. Batangas adds the orange hue of annatto; Laguna likes hers yellowish and piquant with turmeric. Zamboanga's *adobo* is thick with coconut cream.

Three other items represent mainstream tastes and might be called "national" dishes. *Sinigang*, the lightly boiled, slightly sour soup, has a broth as tart as the heart (or taste buds) desires. An array of souring agents—unripe guavas; tamarind leaves and flowers; *kamias*; tomatoes—help make a home-cooked *sinigang* of seafood or meat and vegetables as varied as the 7,000 islands.

There is the stew known as *dinuguan*—basically pig blood and innards simmered with vinegar and hot peppers. Most regions do the *dinuguan* stew in their own versions.

Finally there's *lechon*, the whole roast pig or piglet, star of many fiesta occasions. *Lechon* is slowly roasted over live coals, basted regularly—and made crisp and luscious. The tasty sauce is concocted from the pig's liver, simmered with vinegar, sugar and herbs.

The spicy and delicious sausages from Lucban.

From the surrounds of Laguna de Bay, the heart-shaped lake of the Southern Tagalog provinces, a rustic and honest cuisine has evolved. The lake and the mountains are the sources for: carp cooked in a sour soup; tilapia stuffed with tamarind leaves; and lake shrimp simmered in thick coconut cream.

Farther south, Batangas waters provide many fish for the table: Ocean tuna is layered and slowly cooked in an earthenware pot; freshwater sardines come from Taal Lake; and fermented fish *bagoong* comes from Balayan town. Batangas province

is renowned, too, for its beef industry, its *bulalo* (oxtail soup including the bone marrow) and her strong *barako* coffee (robusta). In Quezon the preferred meat is *carabao* (water buffalo), stewed in a spicy tomato sauce. And the preferred noodle dish is *pancit habhab*—noodles scooped into a banana leaf pocket and eaten like an ice cream cone.

The Bicol Region—six provinces along the southeastern peninsula of Luzon—is a lush land famous for the majestic Mayon Volcano; the smallest fish in the world; coconut forests; *pili* nuts—and spicy-hot coconut-creamy food! It has been oft said that the Bicolano farmer, in the face of frequent typhoons plaguing the region, ties down his indispensable *sili* (chili pepper) plants before looking after his wife.

Bicol is synonymous with *gata* or coconut cream. *Sili* and *gata* come together deliciously, especially in the famous Bicol dish called *pinangat*. Little bundles of *gabi* (taro) leaves are filled with shredded taro leaves and bits of tasty meat; the bundles are simmered in *gata*, and laced with a fistful of chilies.

The Visayas are the big island group in the center of the archipelago, where several cuisines reflect the influence of the Chinese community and the taste of the seas. Iloilo City is famous for genteel households, languid lifestyles—and delicious noodle soups. *Pancit molo* is a hearty soup designed around shrimp-and-chicken-and-pork dumplings. From Iloilo also, the delectable *lumpiang ubod*: heart of palm in soft crepes.

Bacolod and Iloilo share credit for *binakol*, a chicken soup based not on chicken stock but on *buko*, the sweet water of the young coconut. Bacolod also cooked up *inasal*, a barbecued chicken marinated in citrus and annatto.

Down Visayas way, *kinilaw* is at its pristine best. *Kinilaw* refers to the marinating of the freshest fish, shellfish or meat in vinegar or other souring ingredients—for eating raw. In Dumaguete, *kinilaw* is prepared with palm-wine vinegar, lime juice, chilies and coconut cream.

In Mindanao, the frontier land of the far south, everyday cuisine is more Malay in influence and distinctly exotic in taste. Spices are used liberally: turmeric, ginger, garlic, chilies and roasted coconut. Seafoods are eaten raw, broiled or fried; or put in soups with lemongrass, ginger and green papayas; or coconut cream and turmeric. Chicken is served in curry; or combined with taro in a stinging soup.

Root crops are served, alongside the staple rice. Cassava is boiled and grated into cakes; rice appears as *puso*, "hearts", cooked in woven coconut fronds. Glutinous rice is often mixed with shrimp, spices, or coconut milk; or cooked with turmeric and pimento. The most exotic fruits of the country are found in Mindanao: durian, *marang*, mangosteen, and *lanzones*.

Zamboanga is a Catholic town with a distinct Spanish accent on her cuisine. *Cocido*, the traditional Sunday platter, is prepared like its Iberian prototype, with sausage, salted pork, pork ribs, sweet potatoes, corn and cooking bananas. Zamboanga has several very unique dishes— *tatos*, big ugly crabs that taste of the coconut meat they like to feed on; and *curacha*, the weirdest crab with the sweetest flavor.

All Filipinos break bread together on all special occasions, on every minor excuse. The humblest peasant offers to share his meal even with a stranger. With that sharing attitude toward food— so expressive of human bonds—the survival of all Philippine cuisines is ensured.

Picking strawberries outside Baguio, in the province of Benguet. Baguio, which is on average about 50°F cooler than the lowlands, is a popular summer escape for heat-weary Filipinos.

The Filipino Fiesta

*Townsfolk honor their local saints with processions,
music, prayers—and non-stop feasting.*

By Doreen Fernandez

At four in the morning a band marches through the streets, waking the townspeople for the fiesta. Soon church bells ring, calling them to Mass to celebrate the feast of the patron saint—the Blessed Virgin in her many attributes, or saints of the religious orders that worked at the Christianization of the country.

After the church rites, each town celebrates with elements of indigenous and Hispanicized custom: religious processions in which the statue of the saint is borne through town; folk theater like *komedya* and *sarswela*, all free to the public; games (e.g. water buffalo races) and fireworks; and certainly food and feasting.

In the old times, all homes were open to all comers. The town of Lucban, Quezon, dedicated to San Isidro Labrador (St. Isidore the worker), proudly celebrates with food in a unique way. The houses lining the designated procession route are decorated with the varied fresh produce of the area. Rice stalks, bananas in bunches, vegetables, white gourds, squashes, green and ripe mangoes, coconuts, fish-shaped bread, succulent whole roast pigs, and especially the brightly multi-colored rice wafers called *kiping*, decorate, even cover, the facades of houses. The owners compete not only for the cash prize offered by the town, but for the attention of their neighbors, in the promise of another year, the good fortune of another harvest, and the joy of being together as Lucbanin.

This *Pahiyas* festival ends with the afternoon procession which, led by the saint's statue, goes rapidly through the decorated streets, as the homeowners strip their homes and throw the food gifts down to the participants. All day the homes are open to neighbors, friends from other towns, even strangers are welcomed, and the traditional *jardinera* (a meat loaf) is invariably served to all.

In Angono, Rizal, a lakeside town, the celebration is water-based. For the November feast of San Clemente, each *barangay* rehearses a set of marchers: women and girls in native garb (a different color per village), wearing wooden clogs and

Opposite:
The festival of Ati-Atihan in the Visayan province of Aklan draws crowds of visitors who come to revel in the colorful celebrations. Like many other Filipino fiestas, Ati-Atihan represents a blend of both pagan and Christian beliefs.

Left:
The streets of Lucban during the Pahiyas harvest fiesta.

carrying miniature paddles. With several marching bands from Angono and neighboring towns, they stomp through the streets in a particular rhythm, followed by men and boys carrying cans of water and laughingly trying to drench bystanders and each other—all the way to the edge of the Laguna de Bay (lake on the shore of the town of the Bay).

San Clemente and his entourage, including the parish priest and a band, are loaded onto a large boat decorated with greenery and taken for a short trip around the part of the lake bordering the town. The priest blesses the lake, the people and the fish traps. Many of the marching participants march, undeterred, right into the lake, musical instruments and all, and follow the boat as far as they can. The return trip to the church is raucous and water-drenched: participants throw water at all comers; houseowners train hoses on them.

Bananas, gourds and tomatoes are not only for eating. Local produce is used to decorate the houses in Lucban during the fiesta of San Isidro Labrador.

With San Clemente safely in church again, the feasting goes on. Every home serves *pancit, menudo, kare-kare,* and usually the town specialty, duck stewed and then fried crisp.

In Pakil, Laguna, the feast of our Lady of Turumba is celebrated with a procession in which only men participate, bearing her through the streets as they dance and sing.

Quiapo, in the heart of Manila, is the domain of the Black Nazarene, a statue of Christ bearing the cross. On his feast (January 9), the district is impassable, with thousands of devotees crowding the streets. Men in the hundreds vie for the honor of taking turns pulling on the ropes of the *carroza* bearing the image. Women pray and pass the men handkerchiefs to wipe against the statue (to bring them grace). Guests crowd at the windows of houses, looking down on the spectacle. And feasting goes on.

San Dionisio, Paranaque, is known for its *komedya* during the feast of the eponymous saint. The good folk of the town believe that the discerning St. Dionisius prefers *komedya* (a full-length play in verse derived from European metrical romances, and featuring adventures in love and war) to any other kind of play, and if the saint is not pleased with the day's offering, rain will fall on the fiesta.

In Silay, Negros Occidental, a recent practice has been to revive the *sarswela* tradition, this time written, scored, staged and presented by the different *barangays,* in a contest that is part of celebrating the feast of St. Didacus on November 13. The musical comedies feature the concerns, customs and aspirations of farmers, fishermen, and urban folk, Silay now being a city.

In the old, more leisurely days, fiesta preparations started weeks before the actual day. The women brought down and laundered curtains and table linen, washed and polished the silver and porcelain. The saints' statues were given fresh clothes and their jewelry (gifts of devotees) was taken out of vaults. Tenant farmers and their wives came in from the farms, bearing provender: pigs and chickens, fruits and vegetables, and offering help. Cooks brought their best-loved knives, and soon the yards around large houses were filled with willing hands chopping, washing, cooking food in vats, butchering and roasting pigs whole, as large-eyed children watched in mounting excitement.

On the day of the fiesta, the large table in the main dining room was laid, edge to edge, with the best the host could offer: a whole *lechon*, the quintessential fiesta dish; in Batangas, whole broiled maliputo from the Pansipit River; in Bulacan delicate milk pastilles in handcut paper wrappers and whole fruits in syrup etched with floral designs; in Ermita, luxurious stuffed capons Spanish style; in Nueva Ecija, constellations of rice cakes; in Pampanga, fat crayfish in sour broth; everywhere, the regional noodles (*pansit*)—all the specialties of the home, town and region. The host would welcome the parish priest, the mayor, town officials, important personages and relatives. He might even go out to the street to coax the guests in. Feasting would go on throughout the day, with many seatings, and changes of menu from breakfast to lunch, *merienda* and dinner. At the end guests and all workers were given packets of food to take home to the unfortunates who could not come to the fiesta.

At the September feast of our Lady of Penafrancia in Naga City, guests from other towns would start coming a week before, in carriages and *carabao*-drawn carts bearing not only guests but servants, bedding and provisions. They would stay with relatives (no hotels then), but set up temporary households. When the feast was over, they might move on to another fiesta in another town, since these religio-social events range through the year. They not only provide evidence of the Christianization of the country, and the industry of friars who assigned saints to each city and town, but also of the communal feeling that binds Filipinos.

The fiesta is essentially thanksgiving: to the patron saint for intercession, to friends and neighbors for help and support through the year, and to God and nature for bounty and survival.

The tantalizing sight of the fiesta table. The lechon, *or spit-roasted pig, takes pride of place in this delectable array of special feast day dishes at the Villa Escudero.*

Eating Out, Filipino Style

In a country where people eat five meals a day,
a flourishing restaurant scene can be expected.

By Millie Reyes

By nature Filipinos are social and gregarious, eager to share their selves—and their food—with family and friends. Whatever their tastes, eating is a favorite way of life, an expression of being alive marked by munching, munching, munching! Every occasion is an excuse for a tasty spread: wedding, birthday, anniversary, or wake; meeting, workshop or prayer session. Any event will do to gather company and top off the affair with food!

Whether at home or out in a restaurant, Filipinos love to eat communal-style, all together in an informal social gathering called a *salu-salo*. The components of a typical Filipino meal—fresh fish or other seafood; chicken, pork or beef; vegetables; hearty soups mixed with coconut and noodles—are arrayed around a large container of steamed white rice. (Meals must include the staple, rice, or else a Filipino feels like he hasn't eaten at all.) The delectable spread allows diners to feast first with their eyes (Filipinos are *takaw-mata*, greedy-eyed!). Then they partake with gusto—with fork in the left hand, spoon in the right—all the better to mix and match and merrily combine the varied dishes with heaps of rice and accents of dipping sauces.

Eating is done frequently. On an ordinary day, there are generally five small but tasty meals to munch through—breakfast; morning *merienda* (10 AM snack); lunch; afternoon *merienda* (4 PM snack), and dinner. Filipinos eat rice from morning 'til night, supported by rice cakes, nuts, and sugary snacks in-between. Plus there's happy hour and the traditional *pulutan* or finger-foods, the sometimes exotic "appetite-ticklers" that accompany the pre-dinner beer. ("Filipinos are always eating, everywhere, even in the workplace!"—says a bewildered Westerner.) Sheer madness?

There's method to this eating madness! Like Filipinos' grace with life itself, Philippine food comprises a spontaneous, flexible affair, based on an intuition for proportions, a native sense of balance, and a wide array of "complementary" flavors. At its simplest, Filipino ingredients undergo several basic ways of cooking—boiling, steaming, roasting, sour-stewing, or going raw, *au naturel*. But native cuisine remains mostly gentle on the palate: redolent with oil and ginger as in Chinese tradition; rich with coconut, as in the Malay; or savory with garlic, onions and tomatoes, as in the Spanish. Compared to her neighbors' fiery or curried fare, Philippine cuisine is a more reserved species: a naive cuisine accented at table by strong-flavored condiments.

What's most unique to the Filipino eating tradition is the *sawsawan*—the mixing and matching of cooked foods with salty, sour or savory dipping

Intramuros, the historic walled fortress-city by Manila Bay, has become a fashionably nostalgic place to celebrate rites of passage, particularly lavish weddings.

sauces, called *sawsawan*. These myriad table sauces in tiny plates turn the bland white rice and the simply roasted seafood and meats into a meal that's sour, salty, sweet-salty or even bitter-sour—as one chooses. The most common condiments are: *patis* (fish sauce), *toyo* (dark soy sauce), *suka* (native vinegar), and *bagoong* (fermented shrimp paste). These conspire tastily with garlic, ginger, red chili peppers, peppercorns, onions, tomatoes, *wansoy* (cilantro), *kamias* (sour fruit) and *kalamansi* (the small, sweet native lime).

The Bistro sa Remedios in Malate typifies a popular style of dining in the capital that celebrates local food in a sophisticated and adventurous way.

In the good old days, hearty Filipino food was found only at home, cooked by homebound mothers! (Eating out to celebrate an occasion meant going together to a Chinese restaurant.) The closest thing to a Filipino food outlet was The Aristocrat by Manila Bay, founded in 1936 by the matriarch Engracia Cruz Reyes. It had started as a rolling store selling *dinuguan* (a dark stew of innards), *pancit molo* (dumpling soup), *sotanghon* (chicken broth with cellophane noodles), *pancit luglog* (a noodle dish with seafood garnish), and their special roast Chicken Honey. Through four generations, The Aristocrat evolved into a full-blown family restaurant—an all-occasion venue with casual dining atmosphere—and a local touchstone: a place

where everyone high and low gravitated to relish eating something that was truly native Filipino.

By the 1970s, family-sized Filipino restaurants proliferated around Manila, many specializing in chicken of varied styles. Customers adjusted to the fast-paced urbanization, and restaurants answered their eating-out needs. Playing on cityfolks' nostalgia for home-style cooking and provincial days, restaurants named Sulu, Zamboanga and Josephine's comprised a new breed in eateries. They focused on traditional seafood cooking (like *rellenong isda*, stuffed baked fish, or *sinigang*, a sour-broth seafood soup)—and usually served their comfort fare with folk-dancing shows! The innovative Grove marketed a daily banquet of the spicy chili and coconut milk dishes from Bicol Province. The traditionally provincial concept of *kamay an*—eating without the use of dining utensils—was successfully parlayed into a popular fad by The Kamayan Restaurant .

Today Manila's restaurant chains provide the "comfort foods" of the middle-class; their traditional cooking styles are declared in their neon-signed names: Ihaw-Ihaw (all- grilled foods); Pinausukan (smoked foods); Bakahan at Manukan (beef and chicken place); Sinangag ATBP (fried rice and more). One popular Filipino restaurant chain, Barrio Fiesta, features a festive rural atmosphere and specializes in crispy *pata* (crispy fried pork knuckles)—and sometimes singing cooks and waiters too.

Along with urbanization came "fast-food centers," corner-to-corner food concessionaires lining the basements of shopping malls. Filipino office workers in Makati or Malate now troop to the nearest air-conditioned fast-food center, where they find upmarket versions of the traditional *carinderia* (diner) or the proletarian *turo-turo* (point-point) stall, where a variety of home-cooked dishes are displayed at the counter and diners point out their choices, which are served along with a heap of white rice.

On the higher end of the market, amid the gentrification of Manila, there's a new spate of specialty or theme cafes and bistros, which are distinctly Filipino in form and content. Eateries don cozy bistro airs, while they present interesting Filipino fare. Some favorites around the city are Cafe Adriatico in Malate, Trellis in Quezon City, Barasoain in Makati, and Ilustrado in Intramuros. Some eateries specialize in the cuisine of a particular region of the islands; Bistro sa Remedios and Patio Mequeni, both in Malate, serve the traditional, delicious and sometimes exotic Pampanga cuisine. Gene's Bistro in

This simple shack in Mindanao sells refreshing drinks to the fishermen. The fare may be simple but the view is stunning.

Quezon City and Cafe Ysabel in San Juan serve neo-Filipino menus, with creative accents of European derivation.

Manila's top hotels have also incorporated authentic Filipino cuisine in their high-priced food outlets. The Manila Hotel has Cafe Ilang-Ilang, Holiday Inn-Pavilion has Cafe Coquilla, and Westin Philippine Plaza has Cafe Plaza, where Filipino chefs' native expertise is amply showcased, especially during regional food festivals. The Makati Shangri-La and EDSA Heritage Hotel also serve some of the finest local cuisine to elite standards.

Any venue will do. When good food is abundant and shared with friends, it is what best exemplifies the true Filipino spirit. One can only burp with joy!

Part Two: The Filipino Kitchen

*New efficient models may have replaced the old,
but traditional implements still retain a much-valued rustic charm.*

The traditional Filipino kitchen is a concept fast-fading in the city; the old-fashioned cooking room exists intact today only in rare provincial settings or re-created house-museums. The indigenous implements of stone, clay, wood or coconut shell, once used widely in kitchens, are now in the hands of antique collectors who have preserved the *objets* for their pleasing forms. But the implements' functions have been taken over by mass-produced tools and modern appliances of the 20th century. From that provincial kitchen—where Filipino cooks created their delectable native dishes—several traditional tools and methods are worth savoring here.

The typical Philippine kitchen was usually hidden from the public view, as it was a small, smoky, and basic affair. The rural kitchen was comprised of several simple clay stoves propped on an ashy shelf, clay pots of different sizes, cast-iron pots and pans, sundry wood and bamboo implements, and food-processing tools fashioned from heavy stone.

Kalans are bulbous clay stoves, shaped to bear a wood-fire in their bellies while they hold the pots and pans over the flames. Small sticks of wood peek through the front opening, while the cooking fire is kept going by well-placed blowing through a bamboo straw (called an *ihip*). It is a labor-intensive process: The flames are controlled by the constant removal and replacement of the glowing coals, perpetually adjusting the heat, depending on what the dish requires. Gas burners and electric stoves have, of course, replaced the wood-fires and **kalans** of old, but the new technology cannot duplicate the unique flavors that emerge from the gentle, hand-tended method.

Palayoks are the red earthenware pots used for boiling soups and steaming rice. (Traditionally, white rice is cooked with banana leaves lining the *palayok's* bottom and a fragrant pandan leaf tucked among its grains just before it's done.) **Kawalis** are the versatile woks made of cast-iron with curved-bottoms; the parabolic pans are used for just about everything else: stir-frying, deep-frying, braising, sautéing or making sauces. The **kawalis** are also used for steaming: foodstuffs are wrapped in *buri* or banana leaves and propped

Opposite: *The traditional* kusina *or kitchen. Cooking was done on the bulbous woodfire stove in the corner.*
Left: *Carved wooden block used to imprint a pattern on cookies. The carvings on these cookie molds were usually floral or abstract patterns, or sometimes images of saints.*
Below: *Traditional bamboo basket with a variety of uses: storing food, carrying lunch, the trip to the market.*

---

over boiling water. The giant metal pans called **kawas** are usually brought out for fiestas, when the communal cooking is done outdoors over open fires. Baking a native cake like the *bibingka* is done by setting hot coals over and under a clay pot lined inside with banana leaves. And drinking water was kept cool in **bangas**—large earthenware vats. Such native kitchenware is being overtaken by teflon pans and electric rice cookers which transmit new efficiency, but bypass the old country flavors.

Some native cooking implements are still sought after today for both their functionality and aesthetic form. The **almirez** is a stone or marble mortar-and-pestle, indispensable for pounding garlic and spices and for extracting juice from shrimp heads. There are also the rustic **sandok**, a wood-handled ladle with coconut-shell scoop, and the **sianse**, a wooden spatula used for food-turning and searing meats. The **gilingan** is a heavy round millstone used for grinding rice into flour (it now serves as rustic decor). A traditional cook's most important tool is often the chopping knife and **sangkalan**, the solid wooden chopping block and heavy steel cleaver which does everything from chopping a chicken to mincing meat, from bruising a stalk of lemongrass to smashing garlic cloves.

One of the more picturesque basic implements is the coconut grater, called a **kudkuran**. This usually takes the form of a small low bench, at one end of which protrudes a iron grater with sharp corrugated teeth. The user straddles the wooden seat and

manipulates a coconut expertly, to scrape the white flesh upon the grater. Sometimes the *kudkuran* is fondly called the *kabayo* (horse).

Local implements for making native cakes and sweets trace their names to Spanish origins. There are pastry pots and molds of varying sizes, including the **lanera**, a cooking mold for the egg yolk custard called *leche flan*; the **chocolatera** or **batidor**, a brass pot for whipping and cooking chocolate; and the **tacho**, a two-handled copper pan for cooking jellies and pastillas candies. The **garapinera** is a hand-cranked machine for making ice cream.

With time and the modern American kitchen as model, Filipino households have adopted the conveniences of high technology, while retaining many of their traditional (and messy) methods of food preparation. Thus, there are generally two kitchens in the typical urban Filipino home. The so-called "dirty kitchen" (perhaps a holdover from the outdoor prep-area of the provincial fiesta) is where the kitchen helpers do the basic prepping: cleaning the seafood, dressing the chickens, pounding the shrimp, chopping the vegetables, barbecueing the meat. The "clean" kitchen is where the cook uses his or her modern appliances — blenders, mixers, microwave, rice cookers and teflon pans—before serving up delectable dishes to family and friends. The Filipino kitchen has come a long way from rustic days.

Cooking Methods

The simplicity of Filipino cooking methods lets
the ingredients take a starring role.

The four cooking methods that are the foundation of Filipino cookery are boiling (*nilaga*), grilling (*ihaw*), roasting and steaming (*halabos*); cooking methods that comply with the modern-day demand for healthy food and cooking. It was not until the arrival of the Spanish that sautéing (*guisado*) or frying in oil or lard came into use and that process was Filipinized and added to the basic forms of Filipino cookery.

Boiling, or *nilaga*, is the basis for many of the best-loved Filipino dishes, for example, *sinigang*, the pride of indigenous cuisine. *Sinigang* are soups or very liquid stews in which meat, fish or vegetables are combined with a souring agent. The choice of souring agent—or *pampasim*—is vast: lime, ripe guavas, starfruit, tamarind or even young tart pineapple.

The most famous of the many *nilaga* is *bulalo*, which consists of boiled leg bone containing marrow with cartilage attached, plus meat and lettuce. *Bulalo's* flavor depends on the texture and consistency of the beef, the size and quality of the bone, and the duration of boiling time in liquid that is little else but water, salt and pepper.

The ubiquitous *adobo*, both a specific dish and a method of cooking in which pork, chicken, fish, seafood or vegetables are cooked in vinegar with garlic and pepper, depends on braising and simmering for flavor and tenderness. In the days before refrigeration became commonplace, the *adobo* served as a delicious way of preserving food.

Kinilaw is another preserving process that has produced an appetizing dish that is the Filipino version of the Spanish seviche. Raw fish or shrimp are marinated or "cooked" in vinegar, salt and pepper. Visayans favor using fresh fish while the Ilocanos and Pampangos opt for *kilawing kambing*—goat steeped in vinegar and spices.

The wondrous *lechon* or roast pig, epitome of the Filipino roasting process, could have been borrowed from the Spanish delicacy *cochinillo asado*—roast suckling pig. Or, maybe it was learned from our Polynesian neighbors who roast whole pigs on hot stones.

Steaming is another important cooking method. Most steaming is done in a wok and many dishes to be steamed are wrapped first in banana leaves which impart a subtle flavor to the food and preserve its moisture. The leaf is wiped clean and then softened in hot water before being wrapped around the food.

Finally, there is *ginataan*, the generic term for any dish cooked with coconut milk, of which there are many in the Philippines.

Filipino Ingredients

A guide to the products usually found in the Filipino pantry.

Bagoong alamang

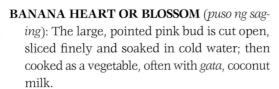

Banana heart

Bean curd

ANNATTO (*atsuete*): Dried, dark reddish-brown seed, used commonly as food coloring or dye. The seeds are soaked, then squeezed in water to extract the red coloring, which lends an orange to reddish tint to food.

BAGOONG A salty, fermented fish paste used as an accompanying sauce, *bagoong* is cousin to *trassi* in Indonesia, *blachan* in Malaysia, *kapi* in Thailand, *mam tom* in Vietnam. Local *bagoong* comes in two main varieties: **Bagoong alamang**—a paste made of tiny shrimp; and **bagoong Balayan**—a thick fermented anchovy paste from Balayan, Batangas.

BANANA HEART OR BLOSSOM (*puso ng saging*): The large, pointed pink bud is cut open, sliced finely and soaked in cold water; then cooked as a vegetable, often with *gata*, coconut milk.

BAY LEAF (laurel): Native to Europe, this thick fragrant leaf is used for spicing sausages and *adobo*; and for giving aroma to stews, beef and duck dishes.

BEAN CURD/ TOFU (*tokwa*): A versatile ingredient made of soybean, and introduced by the Chinese. Rich in protein, bean curd can be steamed or deep-fried, pickled or fermented. Soft white tofu is steamed or added to soups; hard squares of *tokwa* are deep-fried; small cubes of dried bean curd are added to slow-cooked dishes. Red or white fermented *tokwa*, sold in jars, is used as a seasoning.

BEAN SPROUTS (*togue*): Soy beans and mung beans sprout fresh white stalks full of protein (the straggly ends can be pinched off just before use). Bean sprouts are blanched and eaten in salads and soups; stir-fried with other vegetables; or mixed with batter and fried (*ukoy*).

BELL PEPPERS (*siling bilog; siling berde*): The round green or red bell peppers have a sweet, mild flavor and a bright aspect. These colorful peppers are used in fresh salads, in Spanish-style dishes, or stews.

BITTER MELON (S:*amargoso; ampalaya*): A highly nutritious green "melon", this cylindrical "wrinkled" vegetable carries a distinctive bitter taste—which you love or hate. *Ampalaya* or bitter melon stands alone; or in the Ilocano *pinakbe*t.

BOTTLE GOURD (*upo*): The pale and mild bottle-shaped vegetable-fruit hangs long on a vine, until it is plucked and cooked for soups.

CASSAVA (*kamoteng kahoy*): A brown-barked tuber similar to taro. The starchy white meat is steamed and eaten plain with sugar; or grated and mashed into the basic "flour" of native delicacies like *suman* and *bibingka*.

CHAYOTE (*sayote*): This type of squash looks like a light green cucumber, having an oval shape and a small white seed. A good substitute is zucchini. Also called christophene.

CHILI PEPPER (*sili*): Chilies come in two basic varieties: the small and very hot peppers called *siling labuyo*, which are often chopped and used in dipping sauces; and the long flat finger-length cooking pepper called *siling mahaba*, often cooked with soups like *sinigang* or *paksiw*. Hot chilies are used sparingly—with the amount of heat increasing as the size diminishes, and as the color matures toward red. To reduce the heat of a *sili* while retaining the flavor, remove the seeds.

CHINESE CELERY (*kinchay*): A tiny light green leaf that works more like an herb than a vegetable. *Kinchay* provides an intense celery-like flavor and garnishes a wide number of dishes, usually those of Chinese origin.

CHINESE SAUSAGE (*Longaniza; longganisa*): Short, thick and sweet pork sausages, mottled with fat and paprika for the red color. Makes a popular breakfast food; the breakfast plate called *longsilog* refers to its ingredients of *longganisa* (pork sausage), *sinangag* (fried rice) and *itlog* (fried egg).

CILANTRO (*wansoy*): Also called "Chinese parsley." The tiny, serrated cilantro leaves bring an exotic, peppery flavor to any dish. Used in soups; or mixed with tomatoes, onions and *patis* as a dipping sauce for fish.

COCONUT (*niyog*): A complete food and a versatile ingredient. Fresh young coconut (*buko*) provides a refreshing juice and sweet white flesh. A mature coconut (*niyog*) is grated, then squeezed with water to make coconut milk (*gata*)—two separate extracts serve for cooking and finishing. Coconut milk is the basis of those creamy-hot recipes of the Bicol region. Canned coconut milk is available wherever Asian food is sold. Skim off the thicker solids from the top of the cans for "coconut cream."

CORNSTARCH Also known as cornflour, this fine white powder is widely used to thicken sauces. Mix cornstarch with an equal amount of water, add to the pan and cook, stirring constantly for a few seconds, until the sauce thickens and clears in color.

Chinese celery

Chinese sausages

Cilantro

Coconut

Heart of palm

Jicama

Kamias

Lemongrass

EGGPLANT (*talong*): The native eggplant comes in a slender purple-skinned variety. *Talong* is usually grilled over the stove before it becomes a salad; or stuffed like an omelet (*rellenong talong*); or sautéed into a mixed vegetable dish like *pinakbet*.

FISH SAUCE (*patis*): A thin, amber-colored sauce made from boiled, salted and fermented fish or shrimp. *Patis* is called *nuoc mam* in Vietnam and *nam pla* in Thailand. *Patis* flavors every simple dish to taste "Filipino."

GARLIC (*bawang*): A basic ingredient widely used for sautéing and flavoring all popular Filipino dishes. Garlic cloves are considerably smaller in Southeast Asia than in Western countries. Used both as a flavoring and for its medicinal qualities, garlic is often pounded or puréed. (A person who shows up at every party is called *bawang* or garlic!)

GINGER (*luya*): The yellow root of a widely cultivated tropical plant. Often used to add flavor to fish and meats, ginger can be used fresh (with skin scraped), crushed, minced, julienned, grated, dried or powdered. Ginger can be stored in a cool place for several weeks. It has warming, medicinal properties; and makes a favorite Filipino tea called *salabat*.

HEART OF PALM (*ubod*): The white pith of the heart of a palm (coconut or *buri*) is blanched and served as a fresh salad or cooked as a vegetable in the traditional *lumpiang ubod*.

JICAMA (*singkamas*): This crunchy white turnip served with rock salt makes a refreshing snack. Used sautéed as a filling for *lumpia* (Filipino *popiah*).

JUTE LEAVES (*saluyot*): These bright green leaves, rich in iron, calcium and vitamins, are favored by the Ilocanos of Northern Luzon. *Saluyot* gives food a glossy, slimy texture.

KAMIAS The small cylindrical yellow-green fruit gives a sour, acidic juice usually used as a souring agent. It is related to starfruit. *Kamias* is also candied into sweets. Substitute citrus juice or tamarind.

LEMONGRASS (*tanglad*): This lemon-scented grass resembles a leek with its bulbous stem and long layered stalk (one uses only the lower three inches). Cultivated for its fragrant earthy flavor, *tanglad* is peeled, chopped, and pounded; then infused into roasts or soups.

LIMES (*dayap*; kalamansi): A deep green citrus fruit with a tart flavor similar to lemons, the *dayap* is about the size of a small egg, with a greenish-yellow skin; it is squeezed for fresh juice or mixed into sauces. The more popular "native lime" is kalamansi—a small walnut-sized green to yellow-green fruit with an aromatic citrus flavor. Kalamansi makes a delicious fresh juice and adds its lively accent to many foods, from noodles to desserts.

MANGO (*mangga*): The Philippine mango is the succulent heart-shaped "national" fruit that comes fresh or dried, candied or cooked—the perfect golden fruit at meal's end. When plucked green and unripe, the mango is finely sliced and treated like a crunchy vegetable—eaten with *bagoong* (fermented fish-paste) or mixed in with salads. The ripe mango graces the finest jams, ice creams and desserts.

MISO A paste of fermented soybeans. Often used in Japanese cuisine, particularly soups; it is prized for its nutritional value and flavor.

MUSHROOMS Several varieties are used in Filipino cooking, including the expensive dried black Chinese mushrooms (which are soaked in warm water before cooking); and the curly black wood-fungus mushrooms (*tengang daga*) that go into clear noodle soups like *sotanghon*. Button mushrooms are also plentiful.

MUSTARD GREENS (*mustasa*): The thick, white and slightly bitter-tart leaves make an interesting vegetable or a hearty soup, especially when teamed up with ham or bacon.

NAPA CABBAGE (*pechay*): A leafy vegetable with soft, large, green leaves and white petioles, widely-grown in the Philippines. Found in most popular soups.

NOODLES (*pansit*): There's a wide range of noodles, made from rice or wheat flour or mung beans. Among Filipinos, the most popular varieties are fresh egg noodles (*kanton*)—thick round yellow noodles made from wheat flour and egg; dried rice vermicelli (*bihon*); and transparent mung-bean noodles (*sotanghon*), also known as cellophane, jelly or glass noodles. *Pancit* is a generic term for noodle dishes, which may be cooked variously as *pancit canton, palabok, buko, Malabon*, etc.

OKRA (lady's finger): This green, hairy vegetable has a mucilaginous quality and can be cooked alone or in a colorful mix of *pinakbet* (native vegetables sautéed with pork and *bagoong*).

PANDAN LEAF (screwpine): The long frond of a pandanus plant, the pandan leaf imparts a unique fragrance to steamed rice; enhances flavors of meats or fowl; and gives cakes and desserts a leafy green hue.

PEANUTS (*mani*): Common groundnuts go into the sauce for *kare kare*,—oxtail stew made with crushed peanuts and toasted rice; or are deep-fried and used as garnish or condiment.

PEPPER (*paminta*): Black peppercorns are used in stewed or roasted meat dishes, such as *adobo*. Without the skin, the same product is the less pungent white pepper, used in omelets, cream sauces or potatoes.

Dried mushrooms

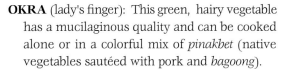

Rice flour noodles

Okra

Pandan leaf

Radishes

Salted duck eggs

Scallions

Spanish sausages

RADISH, GIANT WHITE (*labanos*): This white and crunchy fresh vegetable is often sliced into soups. It is often referred to by its Japanese name *daikon*.

RICE (*bigas*: raw grains; *kanin*: cooked rice): The most basic staple food of Asia. There are dozens of varieties, but the most common forms are polished white rice, the stuff of daily meals; and glutinous or sticky rice for making desserts. Rice grains are simply boiled or steamed in water. Leftover rice is often recycled as *sinangag* (garlic fried rice) for breakfast. Glutinous rice performs in all the sticky dessert-cakes: *puto kuchinta*, *bibingka*, *suman*, and so on.

SALTED DUCK EGG (*itlog na maalat*): The familiar "red egg" is a savory condiment or side dish. Duck eggs are boiled, stored in brine and painted magenta-red. Chopped up with fresh tomatoes and a touch of vinegar, red egg makes a native salad relished with fried fish.

SHALLOTS (*sibuyas Tagalog*): Small reddish onions that add a sweet-pungent flavor to countless dishes. Minced and deep-fried, they are used as a garnish for noodles or soups; they are also pickled or mixed into dipping sauces.

SCALLIONS (*sibuyas mura*): The popular green young onion, also known as the spring onion, is used as a basic and plentiful flavoring in soups and a garnish on meat dishes.

SOY SAUCE (*toyo*): Fermented soybean sauce, a ubiquitous condiment in Filipino-Chinese cooking. **Light soy sauce** is thinner, lighter in color and saltier, used as a table condiment. The **black soy sauce** or **toyo** adds a hearty depth and dark coloring to a dish in the cooking.

SPANISH SAUSAGE (*chorizo*): Chorizo refers to any dried Spanish-style pork sausage packed in paprika-flavored lard. Used for flavoring dishes such as *cocido* or *pochero*, it is usually added to stews, rather than eaten on its own.

SPRING ROLL WRAPPER (*lumpia* wrapper): A thin crepe made from a batter of rice flour, water and salt, the *lumpia* wrapper is steamed and dried in the sun; then used to wrap a variety of spring rolls. The rice wrapper must be moistened with a wet cloth before using, for greater flexibility. Can be fried too, as in *lumpiang* Shanghai.

STARFRUIT (*balimbing*): Sometimes called carambola, this pale green acidic fruit is added to soups and made into pickles.

SWEET POTATO (*kamote*): A starchy yellow-golden root that is more versatile than a potato, as it is boiled, stewed, baked, fried or candied.

TAMARIND (*sampaloc*): This bulbous green pod contains a sour fleshy pulp that is the prime souring agent for soups such as *sinigang na isda* or *sinigang na baka*. (It's the closest Filipinos come to Thais' *tom yam*.) Young tamarind leaves figure in local chicken soups; the mature fruit in sweet-sour candies.

TAPIOCA PEARLS The bulbous pith of the sago palm, the clear little beads are mixed into popular native desserts as *halo-halo, guinataan,* or *gulaman at sago.*

TARO (*gabi*): A tuber with many edible elements. The starchy root is boiled in a vegetable soup; or cooked and candied into a dessert. The dark leaves are the prime ingredient of *laing,* the coconut-cream vegetable dish from Bicol.

TOMATO (*kamatis*): Usually the plum variety is used and can be found in many Spanish-derived dishes, tomatoes are used as a basic ingredient for sautéing; or are mixed into fresh salads and dipping sauces.

TURMERIC (*dilaw*): A ginger-like plant whose root is used as a spice and for food coloring for rice dishes. Turmeric is also used to flavor the insides of milkfish before broiling.

VINEGAR (*suka*): Native vinegar comes in black, red and white hues; made from nipa palm, coconut, kaong or sago palm, as well as from sugar cane. White vinegar can be used for the recipes in this book.

WATER SPINACH/SWAMP CABBAGE (*kangkong*): A deep-green aquatic plant with heart-shaped leaves. Full of nutrition and possessed of an excellent flavor, *kangkong* is sautéed with garlic or thrown into *sinigang.*

Starfruit

Taro

Turmeric

Water spinach

PART THREE: THE RECIPES

Basic recipes for stocks, sauces, vinegars and pickles precede those for main dishes, which begin on page 36

Achara • *Green Papaya Relish*

This Indian-influenced relish is a favorite in the Philippines. It is usually eaten as a side dish to accompany fried and broiled fish or meat.

- 1 cup apple cider
- 1 cup sugar
- 1 tablespoon salt
- 4 cups julienned green papaya (or *sauerkraut*)
- 5 garlic cloves, peeled, julienned and cut in half
- 1 cup julienned carrots, cut in half
- 1 green bell pepper, julienned
- 1 red bell pepper, julienned
- $1/4$ pound fresh ginger, julienned
- 1 cup finely minced onion

Bring vinegar, sugar and salt to a boil in a large saucepan. Add the rest of the ingredients. Cover and turn off heat. Let cool. Transfer to a sterilized jar or bottle.

Ingredients

When recipe lists a hard-to-find or unusual ingredient, see pages 26 to 31 for possible substitutes. If a substitute is not listed, look for the ingredient in your local Chinese or local Asian food markets.

Time Estimates

Time estimates for preparation only.

⏱ *quick and very easy to prepare*

⏱⏱ *relatively easy; less than 15 minutes' preparation*

⏱⏱⏱ *takes more than 15 minutes to prepare*

Clockwise from top left: Sweet and Sour Sauce, Miso Tomato Sauce, Liver Sauce, sauce for Heart of Palm Spring Rolls, Eggplant Sauce, Green Papaya Relish, Shrimp Paste, Soy Sauce with Kalamansi and Vinegar Dipping Sauce.

Sawsawang Mangga • *Green Mango Relish*

2$\frac{1}{2}$ cups green mango, peeled, seeded and
    grated or sliced thinly
$\frac{1}{3}$ cup chopped onions
$\frac{1}{3}$ cup chopped tomatoes
2 tablespoons sautéed shrimp paste

Mix all ingredients together and serve.

Note: You can buy shrimp paste that has already
been sautéed rather than doing it at home.

Bagoong Balayaan Guisado
Sautéed Balayan Fish Sauce

1 tablespoon vegetable oil
1 whole bulb garlic, peeled and minced
1 onion, peeled and chopped
2 tomatoes, quartered
1$\frac{1}{2}$ cups *bagoong Balayan*
1 teaspoon sugar
$\frac{1}{2}$ cup white vinegar

Heat the oil, then sauté the garlic, onion and tomatoes. Add the *bagoong* and sugar.
   Add vinegar and let simmer for 10 to 15 minutes.

Sarsang Miso • *Miso Tomato Sauce*

1 teaspoon cooking oil
1 teaspoon finely minced garlic
$\frac{1}{2}$ cup chopped onion
$\frac{1}{2}$ cups finely minced ripe tomatoes

2 tablespoons *miso*
1 teaspoon white vinegar
$\frac{1}{2}$ teaspoon ground black pepper

In a small skillet, heat the oil and sauté the garlic
until light brown, then the onion until transparent
and tomatoes until soft. Add the miso and mix.
Mash the whole mixture with a fork and add vinegar and pepper. Bring to a boil. Makes 1 cup.

Sawsawang Suka • *Vinegar Dipping Sauce*

$\frac{1}{4}$ cup soy sauce
$\frac{1}{3}$ cup white vinegar
3 garlic cloves, peeled and crushed
Salt and freshly ground pepper to taste
$\frac{1}{8}$ teaspoon ground cayenne

Combine all ingredients in a bowl. Mix well.

Agre Dulce • *Sweet and Sour Sauce*

3 cups water
$\frac{1}{2}$ cup ketchup
$\frac{1}{3}$ cup sugar
1 teaspoon salt
1 teaspoon red-hot (Tabasco) sauce (optional)
2 tablespoons cornstarch dissolved in 4 table-
    spoons of water

Mix all ingredients together. Bring to a boil and simmer for 5 minutes or until sauce thickens. Makes
about 3 cups.

Lechon Sauce • *Liver Sauce*

$\frac{1}{2}$ pound chicken livers or 1 cup liver pâté
$\frac{1}{4}$ cup apple cider vinegar
$\frac{1}{2}$ cup bread crumbs, fresh or dried
3 tablespoons finely minced garlic
1 cup finely minced onion
Salt and freshly ground pepper to taste
2 tablespoons brown sugar
1 cup water

If using chicken liver, broil the liver until half done first and then extract the juices by pressing through a sieve or strainer. Then combine the liver juice or liver pâté with the other ingredients in a saucepan and simmer the mixture for about 30 minutes over moderate heat.
Serves 8.

Annatto Water

1 tablespoon annatto or achiote seeds
4 tablespoons water

Place the seeds in the water and crush them between the fingers to release the red color. Let stand for about 30 minutes. Strain the water and discard the seeds.

Annatto Oil

1 tablespoon annatto or achiote seeds
2 tablespoons oil

Fry the seeds in oil for several minutes. When the oil is cool enough to touch, crush the seeds. Let the mixture stand about 15 minutes; then strain and discard the seeds.

Helpful hint: You may also buy the powdered annatto (packaged) or "*Achiotina*" (bottled in oil) at Asian or Hispanic food stores or supermarkets.

Toyo't Kalamansi
Soy Sauce with Kalamansi

$\frac{1}{4}$ cup soy sauce
3 tablespoons kalamansi lime juice or white vinegar
2 garlic cloves, peeled and minced
3 chilies (*siling labuyo*)

Combine all ingredients and mix well.

Sarsang Talong • *Eggplant Sauce*

2 Asian eggplants, broiled, peeled and smashed
$\frac{1}{2}$ cup white vinegar
$\frac{1}{2}$ teaspoon minced garlic
Salt and ground black pepper to taste.

Blend all ingredients together.

LUMPIANG SHANGHAI & CHICHARON

Philippine Fried Egg Rolls, Shanghai-Style & Pork Crackling

PHILIPPINE FRIED EGG ROLLS, SHANGHAI-STYLE

A popular Filipinized version of the Chinese egg roll, usually stuffed with meat, shellfish or vegetables. 🕐🕐🕐

1/2 **pound ground pork**
1/2 **pound shrimp, chopped finely**
1/2 **cup chopped water chestnuts**
1/2 **cup finely chopped scallions**
1 **egg, beaten**
1 **tablespoon soy sauce**
1 **teaspoon salt**
1 **teaspoon ground black pepper**
1 **package egg roll wrappers (sold in Asian food stores)**
Oil for deep-frying

Pork Crackling (left) and Philippine Fried Egg Rolls (right).

Mix pork, shrimp, water chestnuts, scallions, egg and soy sauce together. Season with salt and pepper.

Place a level tablespoon of filling on each egg roll wrapper, roll tightly and seal with a few drops of water. Continue until filling is all used. Deep-fry in hot oil and drain on paper towels. Serve with Sweet and Sour Sauce (page 34). Serves 4.

PORK CRACKLING

A favorite *pulutan* (finger food to accompany alcoholic drinks), especially when it is just cooked and dipped in vinegar sauce. 🕐🕐🕐

2 **pounds pork rind, cut into 1-inch squares**
3 **cups water**
1 **tablespoon salt**
1 **cup vegetable or corn oil**

Boil cut pork rind in water and salt for 30 minutes. On a baking pan, spread out the cooked pork rind and bake at 300°F for 3 hours. Set aside and let cool.

Deep-fry the rinds in a skillet in hot oil over high heat until they puff up. Serve with Vinegar Dipping Sauce (page 34). Serves 6 to 8.

UKOY & KINILAW NA TANGUIGUE

Bean Sprout Fritters & Fish Seviche

BEAN SPROUT FRITTERS

Best when eaten during *merienda* (in-between meals), this snack is also served as *pulutan*. ☺☺☺

Batter:

> 2 eggs
> 1 cup cornstarch
> 1 teaspoon baking powder
> 1 tablespoon Annatto Water (page 35)
> $\frac{1}{2}$ teaspoon ground black pepper

Filling:

> 1 cup bean sprouts
> 12 medium-size shrimp, with shell
> 1 (2 in x 2 in) piece bean curd, cut into
> $\frac{1}{4}$-inch cubes
> $\frac{1}{2}$ pound ground pork
> Shrimp paste (*bagoong*)
> 2 cups vegetable oil for deep-frying

For the **batter**, beat the eggs well; then add cornstarch, baking powder and the annatto water. Season with black pepper.

For the **filling**, place 2 tablespoons of the batter in a saucer, arrange some bean sprouts, shrimp, bean curd, ground pork and $\frac{1}{2}$ teaspoon of shrimp paste on top. Cover with 2 tablespoons of the **batter.**

Heat 2 cups of vegetable oil in a deep frying-pan. When the oil is very hot, slide the mixture from the saucer slowly into the pan. When it turns a golden-brown color, remove with a slotted spoon and drain on paper towels. Repeat with the remaining mixture. Serve hot with Vinegar Dipping Sauce (page 34). Serves 4.

FISH SEVICHE

This dish is similar to *seviche*—uncooked fish and shellfish are marinated in a souring agent and other spices. ☺☺☺

> 2 pounds tanguigue, skinned (sea bass or blue-fish may be substituted)
> 1 cup white vinegar
> 6 tablespoons kalamansi or lemon juice
> 4 garlic cloves, peeled and finely minced
> 1 cup finely minced onion
> 4 tomatoes, diced
> 2 tablespoons finely minced fresh ginger
> 1 onion, peeled and thinly sliced into rings
> 3 red or green bell peppers, cored, seeded and cut into strips
> Salt and freshly ground black pepper to taste

Clean fish and cut into cubes. Marinate in vinegar for an hour. Drain and add kalamansi or lemon juice and all other ingredients.

Chill before serving. Serves 4.

ARROZ CALDO CON POLLO

Chicken Rice Soup with Ginger

A favorite one-pot meal. This "comfort food" is especially good during the rainy season. ①①①

5 tablespoons vegetable or corn oil
4 tablespoons minced garlic
1 (2-inch) piece of ginger, cut crosswise into
    $1/2$ -inch slices
1 large onion, peeled and diced
$1^{1}/_{2}$ cups uncooked rice
10 cups water
1 2- to 3-pound chicken, cut into bite-size
    pieces
$1^{1}/_{2}$ teaspoons fish sauce (*patis*)
$1/_{4}$ cup finely chopped scallion
$1/_{4}$ teaspoon ground black pepper

In a stockpot, heat 3 tablespoons oil and sauté 2 tablespoons of garlic, the ginger and the onion. The garlic is done when light brown and the onion when transparent.

Add rice and sauté for 5 minutes. Add water. Bring mixture to a boil, stirring occasionally. Reduce the heat to a simmer, add chicken, and continue cooking for another 30 minutes or until rice is done.

While waiting for the rice to cook, heat the remaining 2 tablespoons of oil in a skillet and fry the 2 remaining tablespoons of garlic until golden brown. Set aside.

When the rice is finally cooked, add fish sauce and continue cooking over low heat for another 3–5 minutes. Serve in a soup tureen or soup bowls. Sprinkle the fried garlic, chopped scallion and pepper on top. Serves 4.

Helpful hint: The flavor of the soup is improved if it is made the day before it is to be served and let stand overnight in the refrigerator.

TINOLANG MANOK & BULALO

Boiled Chicken with Ginger & Boiled Beef Soup

BOILED CHICKEN WITH GINGER

This soothing and delicious ginger and chicken soup was popularized in the novel *Noli Me Tangere* by Dr. Jose P. Rizal, the Philippines' national hero. ☻ ☻ ☻

2 tablespoons vegetable or corn oil
1½ tablespoons finely minced garlic
¼ cup finely minced onion
1 tablespoon minced ginger
1 2- to 3-pound chicken, cut into serving pieces
Salt and ground black pepper to taste
2 tablespoons fish sauce (*patis*) (optional)
3 cups water
2 cups peeled, cubed green papaya or zucchini
2 cups spinach leaves or watercress

Boiled Chicken with Ginger (left) and Boiled Beef Soup (right).

In a large saucepan, heat the oil. Sauté the garlic, onion and ginger. Brown the garlic and cook the onion until transparent.

Add the chicken pieces and stir well until the chicken is partly cooked. Season with salt and pepper and fish sauce, if desired. Add water. Cover and simmer over moderate heat until chicken is tender.

Uncover the pot and add the papaya or zucchini. Cook until tender. Turn off the heat and add the spinach leaves or watercress. Serve hot. Serves 4.

BOILED BEEF SOUP

A clear and rich-flavored broth derived from a cow's thigh or shoulder bones, including the marrow. Should be eaten hot—a prelude to hearty table fare. ☻ ☻ ☻

2 pounds beef shanks with bone marrow
Water
2 large onions, peeled and sliced
3 leeks, sliced
1 (2-ounce) package dried banana blossoms (available in Asian food stores)
Fish sauce (*patis*) to taste
Freshly ground black pepper to taste
4 (2 inch x 2 inch) pieces bean curd, cut into ¼-inch cubes

Place beef shank in water to cover and bring to a boil. Boil for 10 minutes then remove shank and discard water.

Boil the shank again in 8 cups water until the broth is flavored and reduced to half the amount.

Add the onions, leeks and banana blossoms.

Season to taste with fish sauce and pepper then add the bean curd. Serve hot. Serves 4.

Note: The beef shank is boiled twice to reduce the fat content of the soup.

PICADILLO & BINAKOL

Ground Beef Soup & Chicken Soup with Coconut

GROUND BEEF SOUP

A favorite Spanish-influenced dish that could be served as a soup or stew. ⊘⊘⊘

1 tablespoon oil
3 tablespoons minced garlic
$\frac{1}{2}$ cup minced shallots
1 cup cubed tomatoes
$\frac{1}{2}$ pound ground beef (preferably round)
Fish sauce (*patis*) to taste
Freshly ground black pepper to taste
4 cups water
2 cups peeled, diced potatoes

Chicken Soup with Coconut.

In a saucepan, heat the oil and sauté the garlic until brown. Add the shallots and tomatoes and cook until soft.

Add the ground beef, fish sauce and pepper to taste. Add the water and potatoes. Simmer at low heat until done, about 1 hour; add more water if needed. Serve hot. Serves 4.

CHICKEN SOUP WITH COCONUT

A favorite of President Bill Clinton when he came to visit Manila. This dish originated from the coconut-producing provinces of the Philippines. ⊘⊘⊘

3 tablespoons vegetable oil
6 garlic cloves, peeled and crushed
1 medium-sized onion, peeled and chopped
5 $\frac{1}{2}$-inch slices ginger
1 tablespoon salt and pepper to taste
1 cup chopped lemongrass
$\frac{1}{2}$ pound chicken, boned and cut into 1-inch cubes
6 cups chicken broth (made from chicken bones)
1 fresh coconut, coconut meat cut into 1-inch cubes, and juice
$\frac{1}{2}$ cup cilantro leaves

Heat the oil in a saucepan and sauté the garlic, onion and ginger. Add salt and pepper and lemongrass.

Add chicken and stir. Pour in chicken broth. Simmer for 30 minutes or until chicken is tender. Add coconut juice and meat. Season with more salt and pepper to taste. Serve hot and garnish with cilantro leaves. Serves 4.

PANCIT MOLO

Philippine Wonton Soup

☺ ☺ ☺

Filling:
  1 cup ground pork
  $\frac{1}{2}$ cup shrimp, shelled and chopped
  $\frac{1}{2}$ cup finely chopped onion
  2 egg yolks
  $\frac{1}{4}$ cup finely sliced scallions
  4 garlic cloves, peeled and finely minced
  $\frac{1}{2}$ cup finely minced water chestnuts or
    jicama (*singkamas*)
  1 teaspoon salt
  $\frac{1}{4}$ teaspoon ground black pepper

Wrappers:
  2 cups all-purpose flour
  $\frac{1}{4}$ teaspoon salt
  3 egg yolks
  $\frac{1}{4}$ cup water

Broth:
  1 2- 3-pound chicken
  15 cups water

  2 tablespoons finely minced garlic
  1 cup finely chopped onion
  2 tablespoons vegetable or corn oil
  1 cup shrimp, shelled and deveined
  Fish sauce (*patis*) to taste
  Ground black pepper to taste
  $\frac{1}{2}$ cup finely chopped scallion

For the **filling**, combine all the ingredients and mix well. Set aside.

For the **wrappers**, stir the flour and salt together. Add the yolks and knead with fingers. Gradually add the water and continue kneading until the dough is elastic and smooth. Roll out on a floured board until paper thin. Cut into triangles, with the sides of each triangle measuring about 3 inches. Scoop 1 teaspoon of filling onto each wrapper and fold two corners in. Fold and press the third corner to seal like a pouch. (When using ready-made wrappers, fold two corners opposite each other and then the two others to seal like a pouch.)

For the **broth**, boil the chicken in the water until tender. Remove the meat from the bones, cut into serving pieces and set aside the chicken and broth.

Sauté the garlic and onion in oil. The garlic is done when light brown, and the onion when transparent. Add the chicken broth, sautéed garlic and onion and shrimp. Season with fish sauce or pepper to taste. Bring to a boil. Drop the *wontons* into the broth and cook for 10 minutes. Garnish with scallions. Serves 6.

Helpful hint: The wrappers for the *wontons* can be bought in packets from Asian food stores.

SUAM NA TULYA

Corn and Clam Chowder

A favorite dish from the town of Sulipan in Pampanga province. At the turn of the century, Sulipan, or Apalit as it was then known, was famous for its *haute cuisine*. This delicious version of the soup is from Gene Gonzalez of Cafe Ysabel. ☻☻☻

3 to 4 tablespoons olive oil
1 teaspoon chopped garlic
1 medium onion, peeled and sliced
1 teaspoon sliced ginger
4 to 5 cups *tulya* (freshwater clams: Manila clams) or *halaan* (sea clams: cherrystone)
Fresh corn grated from 2 cobs
4 cups chicken or clam broth
$\frac{1}{2}$ teaspoon fish sauce (*patis*), more to taste
$\frac{1}{4}$ cup chili leaves (picked), or bell pepper or fresh spinach leaves
Ground black pepper to taste

Heat the oil and sauté the garlic, onion and ginger. Add the clams and stir-fry for 1 minute or until shells open. Set aside $\frac{2}{3}$ of the clams. Add the corn and simmer with the broth as needed. Mix constantly until slightly thick. Add the clams previously set aside and the fish sauce. Simmer for another 5 to 6 minutes.

Float in chili leaves or bell pepper leaves and season with black pepper and more fish sauce to taste. Serves 4.

SINANGAG, LONGGANISA & FRIED BIYA

Philippine Fried Rice, Philippine Sausage and Fried Biya

Rice is the staple food of Filipinos and no meal is complete without it. It is combined here with two other dishes to create the classic Filipino breakfast. The sausage and dried fish can be bought at specialty Asian grocery stores.

PHILIPPINE FRIED RICE ☻☻☻

4 tablespoons vegetable or corn oil
2 tablespoons minced garlic
$1/4$ cup minced shallots
4 cups cold cooked rice (refrigerated leftover rice) mashed lightly with $1/2$ cup water
1 tablespoon soy sauce
1 teaspoon salt
$1/4$ teaspoon ground black pepper

Philippine Sausage (top), Philippine Fried Rice (middle) and Fried Biya (left).

In a 10-inch frying pan, heat the oil and fry the garlic until light brown. Add shallots, rice, soy sauce, salt and pepper.

Stir the mixture constantly to prevent it from sticking to the pan and to ensure even cooking. Cook and continue stirring for 10 minutes. Serve hot. Serves 6 to 8.

PHILIPPINE SAUSAGE ☻☻☻

2 pounds ground pork
$1/2$ cup white vinegar
2 tablespoons minced garlic
$1/2$ teaspoon ground black pepper
Hog casing (available in Asian food stores or Filipino markets)

In a large bowl, mix all the ingredients together. Stuff into hog casings and twist to make links 2–3 inches long.

Hang or dry in a cool place or cook at once, if desired. Prick the skin before boiling and fry in the sausages' own fat. Serves 8.

FRIED BIYA (GOBY) ☻☻

1 pound *biya* fish (or goby)
$1/2$ cup salt
$1/2$ teaspoon ground black pepper
2 tablespoons vegetable oil

Rub the fish with the salt and pepper and let dry for 3 days.

Heat the oil and fry fish for 1 minute on either side or until both sides are browned. Serves 4.

PAELLA

A Filipino adaptation of the famous Valencian dish. ☺☺☺

1 2-pound fryer chicken
1 2-pound pork tenderloin
1 pound large shrimp
Salt and pepper to taste
3 large crabs
20 fresh littleneck clams
6 cups water (optional)
½ cup olive oil
½ teaspoon paprika
2 tablespoons chopped garlic
½ cup chopped onion
2 *chorizos de Bilbao* or pepperoni sausages, sliced thin
3 cups raw rice (glutinous or sticky rice if available)
½ cup canned, puréed tomatoes
1 small bay leaf
1 green bell pepper, cored, seeded and sliced into 1-inch square pieces
¼ teaspoon saffron mixed with 1 teaspoon water
1 cup frozen peas
2 pieces pimento, cut into 1-inch squares
2 hard-cooked eggs

Cut chicken and pork into $1\frac{1}{2}$-inch pieces. Shell shrimp and devein, leaving tails on; dredge with salt and pepper. Boil crabs and quarter. Crack shells or crab claws and set aside. Boil clams in the 6 cups water until they open. Remove empty top shells and set aside. Reserve 6 cups of the clam broth. Preheat oven to 350°F.

Heat the olive oil in a large pan and add the chicken, pork, paprika, garlic, onion and *chorizo* or pepperoni. Toss for a few minutes and add the rice. Stir until the rice is slightly brown. Add the puréed tomatoes, broth from the clams, bay leaf, salt and pepper and stir for a few minutes. Add the shrimp and bell pepper and saffron. Bring to a boil.

Transfer to a serving casserole and bake covered at 350°F for 30 minutes. Uncover the casserole and arrange the clams, crabs, peas and pimento on top. Cover and bake for 5 minutes. Decorate the top with slices of hard-cooked eggs before serving. Serves 6.

ARROZ A LA CUBANA

Cuban-Style Rice

A rice dish with Cuban influence using plantains and fried eggs. ☺☺☺

3 tablespoons vegetable or corn oil
1 tablespoon minced garlic
¼ cup minced shallots
½ cup diced tomatoes
½ pound ground beef
½ pound ground pork
3 tablespoons soy sauce
¼ cup raisins
½ teaspoon salt
¼ teaspoon ground black pepper
½ cup peas
5 tablespoons peanut oil
3 ripe plantains, peeled and sliced
6 eggs
5 cups freshly cooked rice, kept warm

In a large stockpot, heat 3 tablespoons of vegetable or corn oil and sauté the garlic until light brown in color. Add the minced shallots and cook until transparent.

Add the diced tomatoes and cook for 5 minutes. Stir in the ground beef, the pork and the soy sauce. Cook until the meat is brown. Add the raisins, salt and pepper and stir constantly. Add the peas and simmer for another 5 minutes.

In a separate skillet, heat 3 tablespoons peanut oil and fry the plantain slices. Remove from the heat and set aside. Put 2 more tablespoons peanut oil in the pan and fry the eggs sunny-side up. Set aside.

On a large serving platter, arrange the cooked rice with the meat in the center. Top with the fried eggs and surround the sides of the platter with the fried plantains. Serve hot. Serves 6.

SOTANGHON

Chicken Vermicelli

Noodles signify long life and Filipinos consume an abundance of them. This is another popular Chinese-influenced dish, in which cellophane noodles are the main ingredient. ① ① ①

Chicken broth:
  1 2½ to 3-pound chicken
  2 bay leaves
  1 teaspoon peppercorns
  1 cup minced onion
  Liquid from mushrooms

  3 tablespoons cooking oil
  1 tablespoon finely minced garlic
  ½ cup minced onion
  ½ cup dried Chinese mushrooms (soak in 2 cups warm water, strain and reserve liquid)
  ½ cup Annatto Water (page 35)
  ½ cup julienned carrots
  ½ cup julienned leeks
  ¼ cup julienned celery leaves
  ½ pound cellophane noodles (*sotanghon*), soaked in water and when soft, cut into 6-inch lengths
  Fish sauce (*patis*) to taste
  Ground black pepper to taste
  1 cup finely minced scallions

To make the **broth**, boil the chicken, bay leaves, peppercorns, water from mushrooms, and 1 cup minced onion in a stockpot until chicken is tender. Set aside and let cool. Strain the broth through a sieve. Set aside. Remove all the flesh from the boiled chicken. Discard the skin and cut the chicken meat into thin strips.

In a wok or frying pan, heat the oil and sauté garlic and ½ cup onion until transparent. Stir in the chicken. Add the annatto water and 3 cups of chicken broth and bring to a boil over high heat. Stir in the carrots, leeks and celery leaves and cook for 3 minutes. Add the cellophane noodles. Add the fish sauce and pepper to taste. Garnish with scallions. Serves 6.

PANCIT CANTON

Canton-Style Noodles

A favorite noodle dish, to which meats and vegetables are added. Named after the city of Canton, but you won't find this dish there. ☺☺☺

½ pound shrimp, peeled and deveined
1 egg white
2 tablespoons cornstarch
1 boneless chicken breast, sliced into strips
3 tablespoons oil
3 garlic cloves, peeled and crushed
1 onion, peeled and chopped
Fish sauce (*patis*) or soy sauce to taste
Ground black pepper to taste
2 chicken livers, boiled and sliced
1½ cups chicken broth
1 cup dried, black mushrooms, soaked in warm water for 20 minutes, then cut into strips and stems removed
1 small carrot, sliced into rounds
2 tablespoons cornstarch dissolved in ¼ cup water
1 (½-pound) package dried Chinese egg noodles
Kalamansi lime or lemons, cut in halves

In a bowl, combine the shrimp, egg white and 1 tablespoon cornstarch. Coat the chicken strips with the remaining tablespoon of cornstarch. Set aside.

In a wok or saucepan, heat the oil, then sauté the garlic and onion. Add the shrimp and chicken. Stir-fry for a few minutes, then season to taste. Add the liver.

Pour in the broth. Bring to a boil, then add all the vegetables. Cook until tender but still crisp. Thicken with the cornstarch solution. Stir in the noodles and cook until done. Serve on a platter surrounded with kalamansi or lemon halves. Serves 6.

PANCIT BUKO

Fresh Coconut Noodles

Fresh coconut is used instead of noodles in this reinterpretation of the traditional *pancit* by Lito Dalangin at the Villa Escudero. ⏂⏂⏂

1 teaspoon cooking oil
1 teaspoon finely minced garlic
$^1/_2$ cup finely minced onion
$^1/_2$ cup sliced chicken
$^1/_2$ cup sliced pork belly
$^1/_2$ cup shrimp, shelled and deveined
$^1/_2$ cup sliced green beans
$^1/_2$ cup sliced carrots
1 tablespoon fish sauce (*patis*)
$^1/_4$ teaspoon ground black pepper
1 tablespoon Annatto Oil (page 35)
$^1/_2$ cup chicken broth
$1^1/_2$ cups shredded fresh coconut
2 stalks fresh Chinese cabbage
1 cup shredded green cabbage

Heat the oil in a saucepan and sauté the garlic until brown and onion until transparent. Add the chicken and pork and fry until slightly brown.

Add the shrimp, beans and carrots. Stir and season with fish sauce and pepper. Stir in the annatto oil.

Pour in the broth and bring to a boil. Add the coconut and both kinds of cabbage and cook until the vegetables are done but still crisp. Serve hot. Serves 4.

ESCABECHE

Sweet and Sour Fish

A popular Spanish-Chinese fish concoction, adapted by the Filipinos using local ingredients. ☺☺☺

2 pounds red snapper, fish left whole (sea bass, bluefish or carp may be substituted)
1⅓ tablespoons salt
½ cup white vinegar
1 cup water
½ cup brown sugar
4 tablespoons vegetable or corn oil
6 tablespoons minced garlic
1 cup chopped onion
4 tablespoons ginger, julienned
1 cup sliced button mushrooms
½ cup julienned bell pepper
½ cup julienned celery
½ cup julienned carrot
½ cup julienned scallions
1 tablespoon sifted flour

Clean fish and slit open. Season with 1 tablespoon salt inside and out. Mix the vinegar, water, sugar and remaining salt together. Set aside.

In a medium skillet, heat the oil and fry the fish. Remove the fish from the pan and set aside.

In the same skillet, sauté the garlic until light brown, then sauté the onion until transparent. Add the ginger. Add the vinegar mixture. When the mixture boils, add the fried fish, mushrooms, pepper, celery, carrot, scallions and flour to thicken. Cover the skillet and simmer for 5 minutes. Serve hot. Serves 4.

RELLENONG ALIMANGO & ADOBONG HIPON SA GATA

Stuffed Crab & Shrimp Adobo in Coconut Milk

STUFFED CRAB

Rellenado is a culinary technique inherited from Spain. This dish, created by Lynn Sunico of Skyline Restaurant, highlights the delicacy and richness of the shellfish. ⊘⊘⊘

4 to 5 *alimasag* (native crabs) (blue or rock crabs may be substituted)
2 onions, finely minced
8 garlic cloves , finely minced
1 pound ground pork
4 eggs
Salt and ground black pepper to taste
Oil for frying

Fish Cooked with Vinegar and Ginger (top), recipe page 116, and Shrimp Adobo in Coconut Milk (below).

Steam the crabs. Remove shells and flake the meat. Do not remove the claws and legs.

In a mixing bowl, combine the crabmeat, onion, garlic, pork, 1 egg, salt and pepper. Return the mixture to the shells.

Beat the other eggs and dip the crab shells into the beaten egg. Fry in small amount of oil until golden brown. Serves 4.

SHRIMP ADOBO IN COCONUT MILK

A variation of the *adobo* popular in the Bicol region, this time cooked with coconut milk ⊘⊘

Marinade:
$1/2$ cup white vinegar
$1/4$ cup water
$1/8$ teaspoon ground black pepper
1 tablespoon finely minced garlic
Fish sauce (*patis*) to taste

1 pound large fresh shrimp in shell
1 (12-ounce) can coconut milk
3 garlic cloves, slivered and fried

In a medium-sized stockpot, prepare the **marinade** by combining the ingredients. Add the shrimp and let stand for 1 hour.

Remove the shrimp and boil the marinade in the same pot, with the lid removed, for 5 minutes.

Stir in the coconut milk and allow the sauce to thicken; this takes about 15 minutes. Once the sauce has thickened, add the shrimp. Bring to a boil and then remove from the heat. Serve hot, garnished with the fried garlic. Serves 2.

PESANG DALAG & SINIGANG NA SUGPO

Fish Stew & Sour Shrimp Stew

FISH STEW

The success of this simple fish stew depends on the freshness of the fish and the ginger. ☯☯

- 3 cups rice water (Mix 3 cups of water with 1 cup of rice. Strain, reserving rice water)
- 2 inches fresh ginger root, peeled and julienned
- 10 peppercorns, crushed
- 1 small onion, peeled and quartered
- ¹/₂ cup leeks or scallions, sliced
- 1 green cabbage, quartered
- 1 bunch Chinese or Romaine lettuce, cut into 3-inch pieces
- 2 teaspoons vegetable oil
- 2 teaspoons salt
- Fish sauce (*patis*) to taste
- Ground black pepper to taste
- 1 pound mudfish or grouper, filleted

Boil rice water, ginger and peppercorns together for 3 minutes. Add the vegetables and simmer for 3 minutes. Add the oil, salt, fish sauce, ground pepper and let boil for another 2 minutes. Add the fish and simmer for 3 minutes. Serve with Miso Tomato Sauce (page 34). Serves 2.

Clockwise from left: Fish Stew, Sour Shrimp Stew, soy sauce, and Miso Tomato Sauce. Recipe for Miso Tomato Sauce on page 34.

SOUR SHRIMP STEW

Sinigang uses sour ingredients such as tamarind or lemon to stimulate the appetite. ☯☯

- 8 cups rice water (Mix 8 cups of water with 4 cups of rice. Mix thoroughly and drain, reserving rice water)
- ¹/₂ cup lemon or kalamansi juice, or one 1¹/₂ -oz package of tamarind ready-mix powder (available in Asian food stores)
- 2 tablespoons oil
- 1 tablespoon finely minced garlic
- 1 cup chopped onion
- 2 cups diced ripe tomatoes
- 2 cups radishes, left whole
- 2 pounds jumbo shrimp
- 3 fresh, long hot green peppers
- 1¹/₂ pounds watercress or spinach
- Fish sauce (*patis*) to taste
- Ground black pepper to taste

In a saucepan, bring rice water and tamarind ready-mix or lemon juice to a boil. Simmer for 15 minutes. In a skillet, heat the oil and sauté the garlic, onion and tomatoes, then add this to the rice water. Add radishes and shrimp and bring to a boil. Simmer until the radishes are tender yet crisp. Add the hot peppers and watercress or spinach. Add the fish sauce and pepper to taste. Serves 4.

LAPU LAPU SA TAUSI

Grouper with Black Bean Sauce

A Chinese-influenced fish dish with a ginger and black bean sauce. ◑◑◑

1 pound grouper or red snapper fillets
1 teaspoon minced ginger
1 cup water
Salt and ground pepper to taste
4 tablespoons cornstarch, dissolved in $\frac{1}{3}$ cup water
Oil for frying

Black Bean Sauce:
$\frac{1}{2}$ cup diced bean curd
1 tablespoon minced scallion
1 tablespoon minced ginger
1 tablespoon minced garlic
4 tablespoons black beans (sold in Asian food stores)
$1\frac{1}{2}$ cups water
1 tablespoon cornstarch, dissolved in $\frac{1}{4}$ cup water

3 onions, peeled and cut in wedges
3 tomatoes, cut in wedges
1 teaspoon sesame oil

Soak the fillets and 1 teaspoon ginger in 1 cup water for 20 minutes. Remove fillets and season with salt and pepper. Roll in cornstarch-water mixture.

In a medium skillet, heat the oil and fry the fillets until light brown on both sides. Remove and set aside.

To make the **sauce:** Fry the bean curd in the same skillet until light brown. Add the scallion, garlic and ginger and sauté lightly, adding the black beans and water. Thicken the mixture with the second batch of dissolved cornstarch, stirring vigorously.

Return the fish fillets to the pan, and add the onion and tomatoes. Bring to a boil, then lower heat and simmer for 5 minutes. Sprinkle with sesame oil before serving. Serve hot. Serves 2.

MORCON

Stuffed Beef Roll

This delicious dish inherited from Spain is a must for the "fiesta" table. The meat roll is simmered in a tomato sauce until tender. ☺☺☺

2 pounds beef flank steak

Marinade:

2 tablespoons lemon juice
¼ cup soy sauce
Ground black pepper to taste

Filling:

8 (2-inch length) canned Vienna sausages
6 sweet pickles
4 strips bacon
2 slices sharp cheddar cheese
2 hard-cooked eggs, halved lengthwise
1 carrot, quartered lengthwise

4 tablespoons cooking oil
1 garlic clove, peeled and crushed
1 small onion, chopped
1 cup canned, puréed tomatoes
3 cups water
Salt and ground black pepper to taste
Parsley for garnish

Marinate the beef for 10 minutes in the lemon juice, soy sauce, and pepper to taste. Drain and save the marinade.

Spread out the beef flank and arrange the filling ingredients on it in rows lengthwise. Roll with meat grain lengthwise and tie with string.

Heat the oil and brown the beef. Add the marinade, garlic, onion, puréed tomatoes and water and simmer for 1 hour or until the meat is tender. Season with salt and pepper.

Transfer the meat roll to a platter, remove the string and slice crosswise into ½-inch-thick slices. Pour the sauce over the meat and garnish with parsley. Serves 6.

Helpful hint: The beef can be marinated overnight which improves the flavor of the roll.

LENGUA ESTOFADO

Beef Tongue Braised with Sugar

This braised dish, which has a strong Iberian influence, is cooked in wine, spices and vinegar. It is another popular fiesta dish. ☺☺☺

3-pound beef tongue

Marinade:

1 cup water
1 teaspoon whole peppercorns
1 bay leaf
3 tablespoons apple cider vinegar or white cooking wine
3 tablespoons soy sauce
3 tablespoons sugar
2 teaspoons salt

3 tablespoons oil
5 tablespoons minced garlic
$1/2$ cup minced onion
$1/2$ cup finely diced tomatoes
2 potatoes, quartered
2 cups julienned carrots
Salt and black pepper to taste
$1/3$ cup stuffed olives
$1/3$ cup button mushrooms, cut in half
3 plantains, cut into halves and fried

Boil the tongue in a large pot of water for 15 minutes. Drain. Peel off or scrape the outer skin. Trim the root ends and wash thoroughly.

Mix all **marinade** ingredients and marinate the beef tongue for 40 minutes. In a large pot, heat the oil and brown the tongue. Remove the tongue but leave the oil. Sauté the garlic until brown, then add the onion and tomatoes and sauté until soft.

Put the tongue back in the pot. Pour in the marinade and simmer for $2^1/_2$ hours or until the tongue is tender. Add water as needed and prick the tongue to let liquid penetrate. (A pressure cooker may be used to lessen cooking time.)

Remove the tongue and slice. Return the slices to the pot, add the potatoes and carrots and simmer until vegetables are tender. Season with salt and pepper. Add the stuffed olives and mushrooms and simmer for another 5 minutes. Serve hot.

Garnish with fried plantains. Serves 10.

Helpful hint: The tongue can be marinated the day before and kept overnight in the refrigerator.

BEEF SINIGANG

Beef Stew with Tamarind

Sinigang, the quintessential Filipino dish, is any fish, meat or crustacean soured-stew with vegetables. ☺☺☺

    10 pieces fresh tamarind or one $1^1/_2$ -oz
        package tamarind ready-mix powder (sold
        at Asian food stores)
    2 pounds beef ribs, cut into pieces
    5 cups water
    4 tomatoes, sliced
    1 onion, sliced
    3 taros, peeled and halved
    1 pound green beans, cut into 2-inch lengths
    1 pound water spinach, leaves and stalks
        separated, stalks cut into 2-inch lengths
    Fish sauce (*patis*) to taste
    Black pepper to taste

Cook the fresh tamarind in $1^1/_2$ cups water until tender. Mash, then strain to get the juice and set aside. You should have approximately 1 cup of tamarind liquid.

In a saucepan, boil the beef in 5 cups water. Add the tomatoes, onion and tamarind juice. If using tamarind liquid, add this to the saucepan.

Add the taro pieces, and when the taro is slightly tender, add the green beans and water spinach stalks. Season to taste with fish sauce and pepper. Lastly, add the water spinach leaves and cook for another 3 minutes. Serves 4.

CALDERETA & BISTEK
Rich Beef Stew & Beef Steak, Filipino-Style

RICH BEEF STEW

Caldereta, another dish adapted from Spain, is a rich stew of beef sautéed in olive oil and simmered in a tomato sauce. Originally, goat meat was used for this dish, but nowadays, beef, pork or chicken are used as substitutes. ☾☾☾

1/4 cup olive oil
2 tablespoons finely minced garlic
2 cups chopped onion
1 1/2 cups chopped tomato
3/4 cup julienned green bell peppers
3/4 cup julienned red bell peppers
2 pounds beef sirloin, cut into 1-inch cubes
1/2 pound beef liver, cut into 1-inch cubes
2-3 cups beef broth
1 tablespoon tomato paste
Salt and pepper to taste
1/2 cup green olives
3-4 finger chilies (*siling labuyo*), chopped
1/2 cup dill pickles, cubed
1/2 cup all-purpose cream
1/2 cup grated parmesan cheese
1 red bell pepper, seeded and cut into strips

Beef Steak, Filipino-Style (left) and Rich Beef Stew (right).

Heat in oil in a saucepan, then sauté the garlic, onion, tomato and peppers. Add the cubed beef and liver. Sauté for a few minutes then remove the liver. Add the beef broth and tomato paste. Simmer until the beef is tender. Season to taste then add the olives, dill pickles and finger chilies.

Mash the liver and return to the pan. Cook until sauce is thick then add the cream and cheese. Transfer to a platter and top with the red bell pepper strips. Serves 4.

BEEF STEAK, FILIPINO-STYLE

A popular beef dish reinvented with an Asian accent of soy sauce. ☾☾☾

1/2 pound beef sirloin, cut in 6 slices
1 tablespoon kalamansi or lemon juice
1 tablespoon soy sauce
1 teaspoon ground black pepper
3 tablespoons oil
1 onion, sliced into rings

Marinate the beef in kalamansi or lemon juice, soy sauce and pepper.

Heat the oil and pan-fry the beef until medium-rare. Transfer to a plate. In the remaining oil, sauté the onion until tender. Garnish the beef with the onion rings. Serves 2.

KARE-KARE & BINAGOONGANG BABOY

Oxtail Stew in Peanut Butter Sauce & Pork with Shrimp Paste

OXTAIL STEW IN PEANUT BUTTER SAUCE

This truly native oxtail and vegetable stew is accented with ground rice and peanuts. ☺☺☺

3 to 4 pounds oxtail, cut into serving pieces
8 cups water
4 tablespoons oil
2 tablespoons finely minced garlic
1 cup chopped onion
1$^1/_2$ cups Annatto Water (page 35)
$^1/_2$ cup raw rice, ground to a powder in a food processor and dry-fried in a frying pan
1 cup ground peanuts or peanut butter
1 Asian eggplant, cut into serving pieces
10 green beans, cut into 2-inch lengths
1 small Chinese cabbage (*bok choy*), quartered
Salt and black pepper to taste

Oxtail Stew in Peanut Butter Sauce.

Boil the oxtail in 8 cups water for 2 hours or until tender. Set broth aside.

Heat the oil in a large saucepan and sauté the garlic and onion. Add Annatto Water and oxtail to saucepan and bring to a boil. Stir in the roasted rice powder and peanut butter. Add 4 cups reserved broth, eggplant, green beans and cabbage and mix well. Bring to a boil and simmer for 10 minutes. Season with salt and pepper to taste. Serve with *bagoong*. Serves 6-8.

PORK WITH SHRIMP PASTE ☺☺☺

2 tablespoons vegetable or corn oil
2 tablespoons finely minced garlic
$^1/_4$ cup chopped onion
$^1/_4$ cup coarsely chopped tomatoes
1$^1/_2$ pounds boneless pork shoulder or butt, cut into 2-inch cubes
$^3/_4$ cup water
$^1/_2$ teaspoon sugar
4 tablespoons shrimp paste (*bagoong*)

In a large skillet, heat the vegetable or corn oil. Sauté the garlic, onion and tomato until the garlic is brown, and the onion and tomato are tender.

Add the pork and cook until it is brown. Add the water and simmer for 30 minutes. Add the sugar and shrimp paste and simmer for 15 minutes or until pork is tender, stirring occasionally. Serves 4.

CALLOS & LECHON KAWALI

Tripe with Chickpeas & Deep-Fried Pork

TRIPE WITH CHICKPEAS

A local adaptation of a Spanish original. ☉☉☉

2 pounds tripe
1 pound pork leg, cut into 1-inch cubes
6 cups water with 3 tablespoons salt
5 strips bacon
2 potatoes, peeled and cut into $1/2$-inch-thick slices
3 *chorizos de Bilbao* or pepperoni, sliced in $1/2$-inch-thick rounds
1 cup cooked chickpeas
2 (8-ounce) cans puréed tomatoes
2 cups water
Salt and ground black pepper to taste
3 tablespoons diced pimento
1 cup tomato ketchup
Green and red bell peppers, seeded and cut into strips.

Tripe with Chickpeas.

Boil tripe and pork in 6 cups salted water until tender (a pressure cooker may be used for faster cooking). Discard all fat. Rinse the tripe and cut into 1-inch squares. Set aside.

In a large skillet, fry the bacon. Remove and set aside. In the same skillet, fry the potatoes, *chorizos* or pepperoni and chickpeas.

Add the puréed tomatoes, bacon, tripe and pork leg and 2 cups water. Stir, then cover and simmer over low heat for 20 minutes. Season with salt and pepper.

Add the pimento and tomato ketchup; add a little water if the mixture is too dry. Stir to blend flavors and serve hot, garnished with bell pepper strips. Serves 4-6.

Helpful hint: Add 2 inches of fresh ginger to the pot while boiling the tripe and the pork leg. This will help eliminate the strong odor.

DEEP-FRIED PORK

The ubiquitous *lechon*, quintessential fiesta fare, is prepared here by deep-frying rather than roasting. ☉☉☉

3- 4-pound pork belly or shoulder, with skin
3 teaspoons salt
$1/2$ cup freshly ground black pepper
Water
Oil for deep-frying

Season the meat with salt and pepper. In a large pot, boil the pork until tender. Drain and let dry for an hour. Deep-fry until the skin is crisp. Slice the pork and serve with Lechon Sauce (page 35). Serves 4–6.

HUMBA & PAKSIW NA PATA

Pork Stew with Tahure & Stewed Pork Knuckle

PORK STEW WITH TAHURE

A Chinese-influenced dish simmered in a pot for several hours to bring out its melt-in-the-mouth texture. *Tahure*, a type of bean curd made from fermented black and yellow dried soybeans, is available in cans from Asian grocery stores. ☺☺☺

2 pounds pork butt, cut into serving pieces

Marinade:
1 cup white vinegar
$\frac{1}{3}$ cup soy sauce
1 tablespoon crushed garlic
$\frac{1}{2}$ teaspoon dried oregano
$\frac{1}{2}$ cup brown sugar
1 tablespoon peppercorns, crushed
1 tablespoon salt
1 bay leaf

Water
2 (2-inch square) blocks *tahure*, mashed
$\frac{1}{2}$ cup chopped, toasted peanuts

Stewed Pork Knuckle.

Marinate the pork in the **marinade** ingredients for about 2 hours.

Place the pork and marinade in a saucepan, add enough water to cover, then cook on stove. Simmer until the pork is tender. Add the *tahure* and peanuts, then cook until the sauce is thick. Serves 4.

STEWED PORK KNUCKLE

This piquant dish with soy sauce, sugar and bay leaves is another national favorite. ☺☺☺

1 large pork knuckle (about 2 pounds)
Water
$\frac{1}{2}$ cup vinegar
$\frac{1}{4}$ cup soy sauce
$\frac{1}{4}$ cup brown sugar
2 bay leaves
2 garlic cloves, peeled and crushed
$\frac{1}{2}$ cup dried banana blossoms, soaked in water
Black pepper to taste

Place pork in a large saucepan, add enough water to cover and bring to a boil. Add the vinegar, soy sauce, brown sugar, pepper, bay leaves, garlic and banana blossoms. Simmer until the pork is tender and season with freshly ground pepper. Serves 4.

MENUDO & INIHAW NA BABOY

Diced Pork with Potatoes and Chickpeas & *Grilled Pork*

DICED PORK WITH POTATOES AND CHICKPEAS

Menudo, an adaptation from the Spanish word, meaning "tiny", refers to a common, everyday dish of slow-simmered pieces of meat mixed with potatoes. ⊘⊘⊘

$1/_2$ cup diced pork
1 cup water
2 tablespoons vegetable or corn oil
2 tablespoons minced garlic
$1/_4$ cup chopped onion
$1/_2$ cup cubed tomatoes
1 cup diced pork liver
1 bay leaf
Fish sauce (*patis*) to taste
$1/_2$ cup pimento
2 cups peeled, diced potatoes
$1/_3$ cup cooked chickpeas

In a medium pot, cook the pork in water until tender. Save $1/_2$ cup of the broth.

In a medium skillet, heat the oil and sauté the garlic, onion and tomatoes until the garlic is brown, the onion is transparent and the tomatoes are soft. Add the diced pork, liver and bay leaf and sauté for 5 minutes.

Add the pork broth. Season with fish sauce and add pimento for color. Add potatoes and chickpeas. Simmer for 10 minutes longer. Serve hot. Serves 4.

GRILLED PORK

Inihaw or grilling is one of the basic Filipino cooking techniques. ⊘⊘⊘

8 pork chops
1 tablespoon ground black pepper
$1/_2$ cup white vinegar
$1/_2$ cup soy sauce

Marinate the pork in the other ingredients overnight.

Grill over red-hot charcoal and serve with Vinegar Dipping Sauce (page 34). Serves 4.

POCHERO

Savory Boiled Meat

Lynn Sunico of Skyline Restaurant's adaptation of the popular and delicious Spanish *cocido*, a favorite Sunday meal of Filipinos. This recipe includes the *saging na saba* or plantains. ☉☉☉

1 pound pork belly or shoulder, cut into
    serving pieces
1 pound chicken, cut into serving pieces
1 pound beef shank, cut into serving pieces
2 (3-inch) pieces of *chorizos de Bilbao* or
    pepperoni sausage, cut into serving pieces
6 cups water
1 teaspoon salt
1 cup finely minced scallion
2 tablespoons olive oil
3 garlic cloves, finely minced
1 cup finely minced onion
4 cups chopped tomatoes
Salt and freshly ground black pepper to taste
1 small green cabbage, quartered
½ pound green beans
3 small potatoes, peeled, boiled and halved
3 plantains, quartered
1 cup cooked chickpeas, drain if using canned

Boil all the meats in a large pot with the 6 cups water, salt and scallions, until tender. Drain and reserve the broth. Set the meat aside.

Heat the oil and sauté the garlic and onions until soft. Add the tomatoes and continue cooking until tender.

Season to taste. Add the broth, bring to a boil and add the cabbage and green beans.

Continue cooking for another 5 minutes, then add the meat, boiled potatoes, plantains and chickpeas. Add seasoning to taste and simmer for a few minutes.

Serve with Eggplant Sauce (page 35). Serves 6–8.

Helpful hint: To ensure this dish has an attractive, reddish color, make sure you use ripe, red tomatoes. For added color, you can add 1 eight-ounce can tomato purée, or tomato ketchup if you like a slightly sweet flavor.

ADOBONG MANOK & APRITADANG MANOK

Chicken Adobo with Turmeric & Chicken Simmered in Tomatoes

CHICKEN ADOBO WITH TURMERIC AND COCONUT MILK

Adobo, meaning cooked in vinegar and garlic, is the national dish of the Philippines. This *adobo* is enriched with coconut milk and turmeric. ☺☺☺

1 3-pound chicken, cut into serving pieces

Marinade:
$^1/_2$ teaspoon salt
$^1/_4$ teaspoon ground black pepper
1 tablespoon finely chopped fresh turmeric root
$^1/_2$ whole bulb garlic, peeled and finely minced
$^1/_2$ cup white vinegar

1 tablespoon vegetable or corn oil
1 cup thick coconut milk
2–4 finger chilies (*sil-a-top* peppers)
Fish sauce *(patis)* to taste

Marinate the chicken in salt, pepper, fresh turmeric, garlic and vinegar overnight.

Remove the chicken from the marinade. Heat the oil and stir-fry the chicken. Add the marinade and the coconut milk and simmer until the sauce thickens, then add the chilies. Season with fish sauce. Serves 4.

CHICKEN SIMMERED IN TOMATOES

A classic dish with Spanish influences. ☺☺☺

2 tablespoons vegetable oil
2 garlic cloves, peeled and crushed
1 cup chopped onions
1 (2-3 pound) chicken, cut into 8 pieces
1 (6-ounce) can puréed tomatoes
2 bay leaves
3 tablespoons ground black pepper
4 teaspoons salt
1 cup water
5 medium-size potatoes, peeled and cut in cubes
6 (4-ounce) cans pimentos

In a large saucepan, heat the oil and sauté the garlic and onion. Add the chicken, puréed tomatoes, bay leaves, pepper, salt and water. Let simmer for 20 minutes over low heat.

Add the potatoes and pimentos. Continue to cook until the potatoes are tender. Serve hot. Serves 4.

ADOBONG MANOK AT BABOY &
RELLENATO DE PATO

Chicken and Pork Adobo & Stuffed Duck

CHICKEN AND PORK ADOBO

There are many versions of the ever-popular *adobo*, this one is from Joel Fabay, Manila Hotel. ☻☻☻

$1/2$ pound pork, cut into 1-inch cubes
$1/4$ cup white vinegar
$1/2$ cup soy sauce
1 whole bulb garlic, peeled and crushed
1 cup finely minced onions
1 teaspoon ground black pepper
2 bay leaves
2 cups water
$1/2$ pound chicken, cut in cubes

Chicken and Pork Adobo.

Combine the pork, vinegar, soy sauce, garlic, onions, pepper, bay leaves and water and bring to a boil. Simmer until the pork is medium cooked. Add the chicken and simmer for 20 minutes. Serve hot. Serves 4.

STUFFED DUCK ☻☻☻

Stuffing:
3 tablespoons butter
2 onions (one onion cubed, the other quartered)
1 cup button mushrooms, quartered
1 cup ham, cubed ($1/2$-inch cubes)
2 cups ground pork belly

3 eggs, beaten
$1/2$ cup fresh bread crumbs

1 whole duck
1 tablespoon butter
Salt and ground black pepper
Oil for deep-frying
9 cups chicken or duck broth
1 leek, cut in half
2 bay leaves
$1/2$ cup sherry or brandy
1 whole medium size Chinese Napa cabbage

In 3 tablespoons butter, sauté the onions, mushrooms, ham and pork belly until onions are soft. Strain and reserve the juice. Let cool. Add the eggs and bread crumbs when mixture is completely cool.

Rub the duck inside and out with 1 tablespoon butter, salt and pepper and stuff and truss duck.

Heat the oil and deep-fry duck until the skin is browned. Remove from oil and in another pan, braise with the reserved juice. Add the broth, leek and bay leaves. Braise over low heat until the duck is cooked. Season with salt, pepper and sherry. When cooked, remove duck and keep warm.

Add cabbage and braise in the broth until half-done. Remove cabbage and leeks. Simmer the remaining braising liquid and serve as a sauce on the side. Serve duck sliced over vegetables. Serves 4.

LUMPIANG UBOD

Heart of Palm Spring Rolls

☺ ☺ ☺

Wrappers:
3 eggs
2 tablespoons vegetable or corn oil
1 cup cornstarch
$^1/_2$ teaspoon salt
$1^1/_2$ cups water

Filling:
3 tablespoons vegetable or corn oil
1 tablespoon finely minced garlic
$^1/_2$ cup finely minced onion
2 cups heart of palm, julienned, or 2 cups
   canned bamboo shoots, julienned
$^1/_2$ pound shrimp, shelled, deveined and minced
$^1/_2$ pound boiled pork, julienned
1 cup green beans, julienned
Salt and ground black pepper to taste
14 lettuce leaves

Sauce:
$^1/_2$ cup brown sugar
2 cups chicken stock
3 tablespoons soy sauce
$3^1/_2$ teaspoons salt
$^1/_8$ teaspoon freshly ground black pepper
2 tablespoons cornstarch

1 cup finely crushed peanuts to garnish

To make **wrappers:** Beat eggs thoroughly and add the oil. Stir in the cornstarch and salt until dissolved. Add the water and mix well. Heat an omelet pan and pour in a thin coating of batter to make the wrapper. Cook for 1 minute then flip and cook the other side for 1 minute also. Set aside. Repeat until you have made 14 or more wrappers. (Ready-made spring roll wrappers are available in Asian food stores.)

For the **filling**, sauté the garlic and onion in oil. When the garlic browns and onion becomes transparent, add hearts of palm and cook until tender.

Stir in the shrimp and pork. Cook until tender. Add the green beans and simmer for 3 minutes. Season with salt and pepper.

Lay the spring roll wrappers on a flat surface. Place a lettuce leaf on each wrapper, part of the leaf should extend beyond the edge of the wrapper. Add 3 tablespoons of filling. Roll and fold one end. Leave the other end open to show the lettuce (see picture).

For the **sauce**, combine all the ingredients in a saucepan. Cook, stirring constantly, over high heat until the sauce thickens. Let cool.

Brush the rolls with sauce and sprinkle with crushed peanuts. Makes about 15 rolls.

RELLENONG TALONG & BULANGLANG

Stuffed Eggplant & Vegetable Stew with Bean Curd

STUFFED EGGPLANT

A popular eggplant dish with meat stuffing. ☻☻☻

2 medium-size Asian eggplants
5 eggs, beaten
2 tablespoons cooking oil
1 tablespoon finely minced garlic
$\frac{1}{2}$ cup finely minced onion
1 pound ground pork or beef
3 ripe plum tomatoes, chopped
Fish sauce (*patis*) to taste
Black pepper
1 cup dried bread crumbs
3 tablespoons vegetable or corn oil

Vegetable Stew with Bean Curd, picture of Stuffed Eggplant on page 96.

Cut eggplants lengthwise into halves. Broil skin side up until tender. Let cool, scoop out pulp and discard.

Soak skin in beaten eggs. In a skillet, heat 2 tablespoons of oil and sauté the garlic until brown and the onion until transparent. Add the pork or beef and cook until brown. Add the tomatoes, fish sauce and pepper to taste. Continue stirring the mixture over heat until it loses excess moisture. Remove from heat.

Divide the stuffing mixture into 4 portions and fill the 4 eggplant skins with it. Press to make firm and coat each with bread crumbs and then the beaten egg. Heat the oil and fry the eggplants one side and then the other until golden brown. Serves 4.

VEGETABLE STEW WITH BEAN CURD

This flexible, affordable and easy to prepare dish is popular in rural areas and enjoyed by both landlord and tenants at mealtime. ☻☻

$\frac{1}{2}$ cup chopped onion
1 tomato, chopped
$1\frac{1}{2}$ teaspoons shrimp paste (*bagoong*)
1 cup cubed butternut squash
$\frac{1}{2}$ cup fresh fava beans
1 cup water
1 cup bean curd, sliced and fried
1 cup sliced zucchini
$\frac{1}{2}$ pound spinach

Combine the onion, tomato, shrimp paste, squash and fava beans in a deep saucepan. Add the water and bring to a boil.

Add the bean curd and zucchini. Simmer until the zucchini and squash are tender. Add the spinach and cook for another 3 minutes. Serve hot. Serves 4.

PINAKBET & GUINISANG MONGGO

Vegetable Medley with Shrimp Paste & Sautéed Mung Beans

VEGETABLE MEDLEY WITH SHRIMP PASTE

This favorite dish of the Ilocanos in the north is flavored with pork and shrimp paste. ☺☺☺

2 tablespoons vegetable or corn oil
1 tablespoon finely minced garlic
$1/2$ cup finely chopped onion
$3/4$ pound pork, diced into 1-inch cubes
Five $1/2$-inch cubes of ginger
4 ripe tomatoes, cubed
$1/2$ cup shrimp paste (*bagoong*)
$1/2$ cup water
3 medium-size Asian eggplants, cut into 2-inch cubes
2 cups bitter melon, cut into 2-inch lengths (scrape out the soft center and the seeds, first); zucchini can be substituted
10-ounce package frozen okra
10-ounce package frozen lima beans
Salt and black pepper to taste

Stuffed Eggplant (left), recipe on page 94.

Heat the oil in a saucepan and sauté the garlic and onion. Add the pork. Stir and cook for 15 minutes.

Add the ginger and tomatoes and cook for 10 minutes. Add the shrimp paste and stir for 3 minutes. Add the water and bring to a boil. Add the eggplant, bitter melon, okra and lima beans.

Simmer for 15 minutes. Season with salt and pepper if desired. Serves 4.

SAUTÉED MUNG BEANS ☺☺☺

1 cup green mung beans
4 cups water
1 teaspoon salt
2 tablespoons vegetable oil
$1/2$ pound pork butt, diced
1 whole bulb garlic, finely minced
2 onions, finely minced
2 plum tomatoes, diced
3 cups chicken broth
4 tablespoons shrimp paste (*bagoong*)
1 cup (packed) bitter melon leaves or $1 1/2$ cups (packed) spinach

Place the mung beans, water and salt in a large saucepan and bring to a boil. Boil for 30 minutes or until the beans are tender. Drain the beans and set aside.

In a another large saucepan, heat the oil and brown the pork. Set the pork aside. In the same saucepan, sauté the garlic, onion, and tomatoes.

Add the mung beans, chicken broth and shrimp paste. Mix well and bring to a boil. Reduce the heat and add the bitter melon leaves or spinach and cook until just tender. Add the cooked pork and mix well. Serve hot. Serves 4.

GUISADONG GULAY & LAING

Simmered Vegetables with Shrimp & Spinach with Coconut Milk

SIMMERED VEGETABLES WITH SHRIMP

A simple but delicious way to cook fresh vegetables. ⊘⊘⊘

- 1/2 pound boneless pork loin butt
- 3 cups water
- 3 tablespoons cooking oil
- 6 garlic cloves, finely minced
- 1/2 cup minced onion
- 4 plum tomatoes, chopped
- 1/2 pound shrimp, shelled and deveined
- 1 tablespoon fish sauce (*patis*)
- 1/4 teaspoon ground black pepper
- 1 cup carrots, cut into bite-size pieces
- 1 cup broccoli, cut into bite-size pieces
- 1 cup green cabbage, cut into bite-size pieces
- 1 cup cauliflower, cut into bite-size pieces
- 1 cup fresh fava beans
- 1 cup snow peas, cut into bite-size pieces

In a saucepan, boil the pork in 3 cups water; let cool and cut pork into 1-inch cubes. Set aside, and reserve 1 1/2 cups broth.

Heat oil in a frying pan or wok. Sauté garlic until brown before adding onion. When onion becomes transparent, add tomatoes and cook until soft.

Add the pork strips, shrimp, reserved pork broth, the fish sauce and pepper. Bring to a boil. Add the vegetables one at a time, stirring occasionally, making sure that cooking time is provided for less tender ones. Serve hot. Serves 4–6.

SPINACH WITH COCONUT MILK

A popular dish in the Bicol region where spicy foods are common. ⊘⊘⊘

- 1 pound taro or spinach leaves
- 1 1/2 cups coconut milk
- 1 teaspoon minced ginger
- 1/2 cup diced pork
- 1/2 cup shrimp, peeled, deveined and diced
- 1 1/2 tablespoons shrimp paste (*bagoong*)
- 1/2 cup coconut cream (sold in Asian food stores)
- 2 hot green peppers, left whole
- Salt and ground black pepper to taste

Chop the taro or spinach leaves into desired lengths. Set aside.

In a saucepan, combine the coconut milk, ginger and pork. Simmer until the meat is cooked. Add the shrimp and shrimp paste and simmer for 5 minutes.

Add the coconut cream, hot peppers and spinach. Simmer for an additional 3 minutes and season to taste. Serve hot. Serves 4.

Spinach with Coconut Milk (left) and Simmered Vegetables with Shrimp (right).

ENSALADANG AMPALAYA & MANGGANG HILAW

Bitter Melon Salad & Green Mango Salad

BITTER MELON SALAD

Bitter and salty flavors are blended together in this unique and highly nutritious salad from Vincent Yap at The Westin Philippine Plaza. ◔◔

2 cups seeded and julienned bitter melon
5 shallots, sliced
3 tablespoons shrimp paste (*bagoong*)
4 small, ripe plum tomatoes, sliced

Sprinkle the bitter melon with salt and let stand in a colander for 30 minutes. Rinse off the salt.

In a large mixing bowl, mix the bitter melon with the remaining ingredients. Let stand for 10 minutes so the flavors develop and serve. Serves 2.

Bitter Melon Salad (left) and Green Mango Salad (right).

GREEN MANGO SALAD

A salad made with the unripened "Queen of Philippine Fruit." ◔◔

1 cup shredded green mango
1 cup sliced ripe plum tomato
2 salted eggs, peeled and chopped (see below)
3 shallots, chopped

Mix all the ingredients together and serve. Serves 2.

Helpful hint: To make salted eggs, pour $\frac{3}{4}$ cup salt into a saucepan. Add a dozen eggs in the shell and water to cover. Boil for 2 minutes, then transfer the eggs to sterilized jars and add salted water. Cover and leave for $1\frac{1}{2}$ months. Hard cook the eggs before using.

MAJA BLANCA MAIZ & LECHE FLAN

Coconut Corn Cake & Crème Caramel

COCONUT CORN CAKE ⏲⏲⏲

Latik:

3 cups coconut milk

2 cups fresh or canned corn kernels
10 cups milk
1 cup white sugar
$^1/_2$ cup fresh coconut oil (see below)
1 teaspoon toasted aniseed
1 cup *latik* (see below)

Coconut Corn Cake.

To make **latik**: Boil coconut milk until oil is formed, together with a cheese-like precipitate that becomes brown in color—this is the *latik*. Reserve the **oil**.

Blend corn kernels in a food processor with 2 cups of the milk, then strain in a sieve. To the strained corn, add remaining milk and sugar and cook over medium heat. Stir constantly and when mixture begins to thicken, reduce the heat and add the fresh coconut oil, little by little, to avoid burning. When thick, add the toasted aniseed and mix well. Pour into a serving platter greased with coconut oil. When cool, serve with *latik* sprinkled on top. Serves 6 to 8.

Note: Fresh coconut oil is used as an ingredient in some dishes and for greasing plates and molds, while *latik* is used as a topping for local delicacies.

CRÈME CARAMEL ⏲⏲⏲

Caramel:

1 cup sugar
$^1/_4$ cup water

Custard:

12 egg yolks
2 (13-ounce) cans evaporated milk
1 (14-ounce) can sweetened condensed milk
1 teaspoon vanilla extract

To make the **caramel**, boil the sugar and water in a saucepan and stir continuously over medium heat until sugar is melted. Pour the caramelized syrup into flan molds or custard cups, tilting the molds to make sure the whole surface is covered. Set aside.

For the **custard**: Combine the ingredients in a large bowl. Stir lightly when mixing to prevent bubbles or foam from forming. Strain slowly, while pouring into the caramel-lined molds. Preheat the oven to 325°F.

Cover the molds with aluminum foil and place in a larger tray filled with water. Bake in oven for 1 hour or until the mixture is firm. Cool before unmolding onto a platter. Serves 10.

Note: Any ovenware dish about 2 inches deep may be used instead of individual molds.

BRAZO DE MERCEDES

Crème-Filled Log Cake

A mouth-watering dessert of Spanish origins named after the mysterious Mercedes, who was perhaps the lady who introduced this extravagant dessert to the Philippines. ☻☻☻

Filling:

    5 cups milk
    1 cup sugar
    2 tablespoons unsalted butter
    1 tablespoon vanilla extract
    8 egg yolks
    $\frac{1}{4}$ cup toasted and finely ground cashew nuts

Meringue:

    10 egg whites
    1 teaspoon cream of tartar
    1 teaspoon vanilla extract
    1 cup sugar

    Butter

For the **filling**: In a saucepan, simmer the milk over low heat until reduced to 2 cups. Add the sugar, butter and vanilla extract, stirring all the while. Remove from the heat.

Beat the egg yolks in a mixing bowl. Combine the milk mixture and egg yolks in a double boiler over low heat, beating all the while. Stir well to avoid curdling.

Add the cashew nuts and continue cooking entire mixture over low heat, stirring constantly, until the mixture has the consistency of a paste. Set aside.

To make the **meringue**, preheat oven to 325°F. Beat the egg whites, cream of tartar and vanilla together. Gradually add 1 cup sugar, beating continuously until the meringue is stiff.

Line a large cookie sheet (12 in x 18 in) with parchment paper greased with butter and spread the meringue evenly on top in a $\frac{1}{4}$-inch layer. Bake until brown, about 20 minutes, or until set.

When set, remove from the oven and invert hot meringue onto another sheet of greased parchment paper. Peel away used parchment. Spread the filling evenly on top of the meringue and roll into a log. Brush with butter and brown again in the oven. Serves 6-8.

TOCINO DEL CIELO & YEMA

Confection of Eggs and Syrup & Egg Balls

Two wickedly delicious egg and sugar concoctions from Gene Gonzalez at Cafe Ysabel.

CONFECTION OF EGGS AND SYRUP
🕐🕐🕐

Topping:
- 2½ cups sugar
- ½ cup water
- 1½ teaspoons lime or lemon juice

Egg base:
- 4 cups sugar
- 1 cup water
- ½ cup butter, softened
- 25 egg yolks

To make the **topping**, combine the sugar, water and lime or lemon juice in a saucepan. Boil until the syrup is medium brown.

Pour into molds, distributing the syrup evenly to completely cover the bottom of the molds.

For the **base**, boil the sugar and water in a saucepan until the syrup forms a soft ball when a little is dropped into a cup of cold water. Remove from the heat and let cool in saucepan.

When the syrup is cool, mix in the butter and egg yolks. Strain to remove lumps.

Pour into the prepared molds. Place the molds in a water bath with enough water to submerge them halfway. The pan should be tall enough to cover the molds completely. Cover the pan with a flat tray and bake at 350°F for 1 hour, or until a toothpick inserted in the center of a *tocino* comes out clean.

Turn off the heat and let the *tocinos* cool inside the oven. Unmold by passing a thin, sharp knife around each *tocino*. Serves 6 to 8.

EGG BALLS 🕐🕐🕐

Egg balls:
- 36 egg yolks
- 12 whole eggs
- 4 cups sugar

Caramel coating:
- 3 cups sugar
- 4 cups water
- ¼ teaspoon cream of tartar

To make the **egg balls**, combine the yolks, whole eggs and sugar in a double boiler. Cook, stirring constantly, until the mixture thickens. Let cool, then roll into balls and sprinkle with sugar.

For the **coating**: In a saucepan, boil the sugar, water and cream of tartar to make a syrup. Dip each ball in the syrup and let cool. Makes 90 to 100 balls.

HALO HALO SUPREME & BUKO SALAD

Exotic Fruit Mix & Fresh Coconut Delight

EXOTIC FRUIT MIX

Known as the "Queen of Desserts"—this is the country's most popular dessert. Similar to Malaysia's *ice cachang*, it features the exotic fruits and vegetables that Filipinos enjoy. This recipe is from Gene Gonzalez at Cafe Ysabel. ⏲⏲⏲

Base:
> 1 teaspoon sweetened red mung beans
> 1 teaspoon sweetened white beans
> 1 tablespoon sweetened plantains
> 1 tablespoon violet yam (*ube*)
> 1 tablespoon coconut sport (*macapuno* balls)
> 1 tablespoon coconut gelatin (*nata de coco*)
> 1 teaspoon palm nut (*kaong*)
> 1 tablespoon creamed corn
> Ice

Topping 1:
> 2 tablespoons pandan syrup (available at Asian food markets as McCormick Pandan Extract)
> $\frac{1}{3}$ cup water buffalo milk or evaporated milk

Topping 2:
> 1 tablespoon Crème Caramel (page 102)
> 1 tablespoon *pinipig* (rice crispies, available at Asian food stores)
> 2 scoops *mantecado* ice cream or French vanilla ice cream

Exotic Fruit Mix, picture of Fresh Coconut Delight on page 110.

Fill the bottom half of a coupe glass with the base ingredients. Add enough ice to reach the top.

Pour the pandan syrup and the milk onto the ice. Top with Crème Caramel, *pinipig* and a scoop of *mantecado* ice cream. Serves 1.

FRESH COCONUT DELIGHT

A delectable and refreshing fresh coconut dessert from Lito Dalango at the Villa Escudero. ⏲⏲

> 2 cups grated coconut (*buko*) (can be bought frozen in Asian food stores)
> 1 (15-ounce) can fruit cocktail, drained
> 1 (15-ounce) can corn kernels, drained
> $\frac{1}{2}$ cup sweetened coconut gelatin, drained (*nata de coco*)
> $\frac{1}{2}$ cup sweetened palm nut, drained (*kaong*)
> $\frac{1}{2}$ cup sago pearls (assorted colors)
> $\frac{1}{2}$ cup condensed milk
> $\frac{1}{2}$ cup grated cheddar cheese

In a large mixing bowl, combine all the ingredients and mix thoroughly. Chill before serving. Serves 4.

Helpful hint: Most of the specialty Filipino ingredients in these desserts can be bought bottled in Asian food stores.

SAGO AT NATA DE COCO & CREMA DE UBE

Sago and Coconut Blend & Crema de Ube

Two more traditional desserts from Lito Dalangin, Villa Escudero.

SAGO AND COCONUT BLEND ☺☺☺

1 cup sago pearls
$\frac{1}{2}$ cup coconut gelatin (*nata de coco*)
$\frac{1}{2}$ cup sugar
1 piece pandan leaf
$1\frac{1}{2}$ cups of water

Sago and Coconut Blend (left), Fresh Coconut Delight (middle) and Creme de Ube (right). Recipe for Fresh Coconut Delight on page 108.

Cook sago and coconut gelatin according to directions on packages. Drain.

Mix the well-drained sago, coconut gelatin, sugar and pandan leaf in a large saucepan and add $1\frac{1}{2}$ cups of water. Bring to a boil, and simmer for 15 minutes, stirring. Remove from the heat and let cool. Serve cold. Serves 2.

CREMA DE UBE

Ube or violet yam is the basis of this dessert. Boiled and grated, *ube* is made into *halaya* or jam. ☺☺☺

2 pounds violet yam, boiled and grated
2 cups evaporated milk
$1\frac{1}{4}$ cups sugar

Crema:
1 cup coconut milk
$\frac{1}{2}$ cup sugar
$\frac{1}{2}$ cup water
$\frac{1}{2}$ cup condensed milk
$\frac{1}{2}$ cup evaporated milk
2 tablespoons of cornstarch dissolved in $\frac{1}{4}$ cup water

For the **halaya:** In a thick-bottomed pan, combine grated yam, evaporated milk and sugar. Cook over medium heat until very thick. Stir constantly to prevent sticking and pour into round, 2-inch high pan, greased with melted butter. Cool.

To make the **crema:** Cook the coconut milk in a saucepan over medium heat, stir constantly to avoid scorching. When thickened, add $\frac{1}{2}$ cup sugar and cook until it dissolves.

Add water, condensed milk, evaporated milk and the cornstarch mixture and continue stirring until creamy, about 10 minutes. Set aside to cool.

To serve, top the jam with *crema* and garnish with *macupuno* balls. Serves 4.

Helpful hints: *Nata de coco,* or bottled coconut gelatin, and a powdered version of *ube* or yam can be bought from Asian specialty stores. *Macupuno* balls are sweetened coconut balls, also available in specialty stores; there is no substitute.

RICE CAKES

Kutsinta • *Brown Rice Cake*

A favorite snack, especially when served with freshly grated coconut. ☺☺

1 cup rice flour
2 cups brown sugar
3 cups water
**1 teaspoon lye water (potassium carbonate
  solution sold in Asian food stores)**
Freshly grated coconut

*Rice Patties
with Sesame
and Coconut (left),
Brown Rice Cake
(middle) and
Cassava Patties
with Coconut
(right). No recipe
for Suman sa
Lihiya (far right).*

In a mixing bowl, combine all the ingredients and mix well. Pour into muffin pans, until halfway full.

Steam in a large pan with a cover; the water should be 2 inches deep. Cook for 30 minutes or until a toothpick inserted comes out clean. Add more water if needed until cooking is done.

Remove from the muffin pans and serve with freshly grated coconut. Serves 4.

Palitao • *Rice Patties with Sesame
and Coconut* ☺☺☺

**1 cup sweet rice flour (sold in Asian food
  stores under the brand name "Mochiko")**
3 cups water
3 cups grated fresh coconut
2 cups toasted sesame seeds
2 cups sugar

In a mixing bowl, combine the sweet rice flour and water to make a smooth dough.

With floured hands shape the dough into small patties, 3 inches in diameter and $\frac{1}{2}$-inch thick.

Bring water in a saucepan to a boil and drop in the patties. When they float to the top, scoop them out and coat with grated coconut. Sprinkle with sesame seeds and sugar and serve immediately. Serves 4.

Pichi-Pichi • *Cassava Patties
with Coconut* ☺☺☺

**1 cup grated cassava (frozen cassava is
  available in Asian food stores)**
**1 cup pandan water (boil pandan leaves with
  water or use McCormick pandan extract)**
1 cup sugar
**2 teaspoons lye water (available in Asian food
  stores)**
3 cups grated fresh coconut

Squeeze the juice from the cassava and discard. In a bowl, combine cassava, pandan water, sugar and lye water. Mix well and pour into small muffin pans. Steam until soft and transparent, approximately 5 minutes. Remove from pans and roll in grated coconut. Serves 4.

DRINKS

Pandan Iced Tea

$\frac{1}{2}$ pound pandan leaves or 2 tablespoons
    McCormick Pandan Extract (available in
    supermarkets or Asian food stores)
1 pound lemongrass
15 cups water
1 cup sugar

In a large pot, boil pandan leaves and lemongrass in water until the liquid is reduced to half.

Let cool and serve in glasses with ice. Serves 4.

Fresh Mango Shake

2 ripe mangoes
3 cups crushed ice
Sugar (optional)

Peel mangoes and scrape off the flesh, using a knife.

Put the mango flesh in a blender and add the ice. Blend at medium speed to mix the ingredients. Add sugar to taste if desired.

Serve in a tall glass. Serves 2.

Green Mango Shake

2 green mangoes, peeled, seeded and cut into
    small portions
$\frac{1}{2}$ cup syrup ($\frac{1}{4}$ cup white sugar or honey dis-
    solved in $\frac{1}{2}$ cup of hot water)
2 cups crushed ice

Place mango in a blender and add syrup and crushed ice.

Turn on blender at medium speed, gradually increasing speed until the texture is creamy and the ice has been finely ground. Serve immediately. Serves 2.

Salabat • Ginger Iced Tea

$\frac{1}{2}$ pound fresh ginger, sliced
5 cups water
1 cup brown sugar

Boil all the ingredients together. Add more water if the tea is too strong. Strain and serve hot or cold. Serves 4 to 5.

Additional Recipes

Bringhe • *Luzon-Style Rice*

Coconut milk and glutinous rice are the main ingredients of this Filipino poor man's version of paella. ⏲⏲⏲

3 tablespoons vegetable or corn oil
2 tablespoons minced garlic
$\frac{1}{2}$ cup chopped onion
1 3-pound chicken, boiled and cut into serving pieces
1 cup shrimp, shelled and deveined
1 cup pork, boiled for 15 minutes, then cut into $\frac{1}{2}$-inch cubes
2 cups uncooked rice, washed and drained (glutinous rice is preferable)
1 bay leaf
1 teaspoon salt
2 (12-ounce) cans coconut milk
1 cup shelled peas
$\frac{1}{8}$ teaspoon ground turmeric
3 hard-cooked eggs, halved
1 red or green bell pepper, sliced thinly

In a stockpot or large, heavy saucepan, heat the oil and sauté the garlic until brown and the onion until transparent. Add the chicken, shrimp and pork and sauté until brown.

Add the rice, bay leaf, salt, coconut milk, peas and ground turmeric. Stir the mixture to prevent it from sticking to the bottom of the pot. Lower the heat, cover the pot and simmer until the meat and rice are tender. This takes about 20 to 30 minutes.

Garnish with hard-cooked eggs and bell pepper strips. Serves 4 to 6.

Paksiw na Isda
Fish Cooked with Vinegar and Ginger ⏲⏲

$\frac{1}{2}$ cup apple cider vinegar
1 cup water
2-inch length fresh ginger, julienned
1 tablespoon finely minced garlic
Fish sauce (*patis*) to taste
1 hot green pepper
1 pound sea bass (mullet, bluefish or porgy may be substituted), leave fish whole
1 tablespoon vegetable or corn oil
1 cup minced scallion

Bring the vinegar and water to a boil in a clay, enamel or non-aluminum pot. Add the ginger, garlic, fish sauce and green pepper and boil for 3 minutes.

Add the fish and the oil, cover and simmer until fish is cooked. Garnish with minced scallion and serve. Serves 4.

Sources

Page 2: black and white ceramics from Amalia Inc.

Page 39: background painting by Roberto Villanueva (1987), Christine's Gallery.

Page 45: background woodcut by Jordan Mang-Osan, Christine's Gallery.

Page 53: 2 stoneware pieces by Lanelle Abueva Fernando, Crescent Moon Café and Workshop.

Page 55: mahogany deskset, cubes and plate from Osmundo's.

Page 57: crockery by Lu Bigyan, Ugo Bigyan Pottery.

Page 63: mother-of-pearl plate from Katutubo; capiz shell placemats from Tesoro's.

Page 65: freeform plates by Lu Bigyan, Ugo Bigyan Pottery.

Page 69: black and gold platter by Jon Pettyjohn, Pansol Studio Pottery.

Page 77: 2 freeform plates by Lanelle Abueva Fernando, Crescent Moon Cafe and Workshop; water buffalo horn and bone cutlery from Tesoro's; background antique table from Katutubo.

Page 79: square stoneware by Lanelle Abueva Fernando, Crescent Moon Cafe and Workshop.

Page 81: stoneware bowls and plate by Lanelle Abueva Fernando, Crescent Moon Cafe and Workshop.

Page 85: woven placemat, and red food cover made by the Mandaya tribe, from crafts market, Davao City, Mindanao.

Page 93: Japanese-style stoneware plates by Lanelle Abueva Fernando, Crescent Moon Café and Workshop.

Page 99: colored ceramics from Amalia Inc.

Page 101: roughhewn trunk as service platter from Osmundo's.

List of artists/craft stores

Amalia Inc. factory and showroom, Emilio Aguinaldo Highway, Bacoor, Cavite. Amalia ceramics also available through Landmark or Shoemart in Manila.

Christine's Gallery, 236 Chuntug Street, Baguio City, Cordillera.
Tel.: (074) 443-9659.

Lanelle Abueva Fernando, ceramist. C/of Crescent Moon Cafe and Workshop, Antipolo, Rizal.
Tel.: (02) 658-3866.

Katutubo, Artifacts and Crafts. La O' Center, Unit 301, 100 Arnaiz Avenue corner Makati Ave, Makati, Manila.
Tel.: (632) 818-6031.

The Landmark Corporation, Homemaker's Center, Ground floor, Makati Avenue, Makati, Manila.
Tel.: (02) 812-1945.

The Mandayas, an indigenous people from the Davao region in Mindanao, are known for their handicrafts, particularly handloom weaving. Places to buy Mandaya crafts are the Mandaya Weaving Center at the Davao Insular Hotel or among the shops in the Aldevinco Shopping Arcade on C.M. Recto in Davao City.

Osmundo's, Furniture, Art and Antiques. La O'Center, Unit 303, 100 Arnaiz Avenue corner Makati Avenue, Makati, Manila.
Tel.: (02) 867-2075.

Jon and Tess Pettyjohn, ceramists. Pansol Studio Pottery, Glorietta IV, 3rd Floor Unit #344, Ayala Center, Makati.

SM Shoemart Department Store, Homeworld Shopping, 2nd Floor Annex, SM Building Ayala Center, Makati, Manila.
Tel.: (02) 867-4227.

Tesoro's Handicrafts, 1325A. Mabini St, Ermita, Manila.
Tel.: (632) 524-3936
or 1016 Arnaiz Avenue (formerly Pasay Rd), Makati.
Tel.: (02) 843-3169.

Ugo Bigyan Studio Pottery, Barangay Lusakan, Tiaong, Quezon.
Tel.: (63-4264) 49144.

Acknowledgments

The Publisher would like to thank Shirley Bacsafra; David Baradas for loaning us crafts from his kitchen collection; Bonjin Bolinao for her help with the photo shoot logistics; the Bureau of International Tourism Promotion of the Department of Tourism, Philippines; Bobby Caballero; Marla Yotoko Chorengel; Rachy Cuna for his help with styling; Marivic Gonzales; the Gonzalez family; Nissan Motors, Philippines; Theresa Ng; Philippine Consulate General Library, New York; Philippine Department of Tourism, New York; Elizabeth Reyes for coordination of the photo shoot, styling, and her generous help in innumerable other ways; Marie L. Reyes; B. Roxas for delicious food talk in Laguna; Noelle R. Schifferer; Rene Tanoy; Ramon Villegas for the loan of ethnic treasures; Emma Ruth Yulo-Kitiyakara, the Philippines Department of Tourism, New York.

The Publisher would especially like to thank all of the participating restaurants and hotels, and their staff:

Café Ysabel: 455 P. Guevarra St., San Juan, Metro Manila.
Tel:. (632) 722-0349.
Gene Gonzalez; Rizalina Chura; D.J. Deloso; Eugene Raymundo.

Hidden Valley Springs Resort:
Office - Ground Floor, Cattleya Gardens, 111 Carlos Palanca Jr. Street, Legaspi Village, Makati City 1229.
Tel.: (632) 818-4034/812-1610;
Telefax: (632) 812-1609.

Fernando A. Endaya, Chief cook; Joseph A. Albano, Dining-room Supervisor; Victor M. Endaya, Asst Dining-room Supervisor; Benigna V. Roxas; Rebecca B. Roxas; Rafael J. Roxas; Lolita B. Roxas; Guillermo B. Roxas; Judith C. Roxas; Eugenia R. Vallarta.

The Manila Hotel: One Rizal Park, 1099 Manila.
Tel.: (632) 527-0011;
Fax.: (632) 527-0022–24.
Int. Toll Free No. 1-800-9 MNL HTL
http://www.manila-hotel.com. ph
Raimund Braun, Executive Chef; Joel Fabay, Demi-Chef; Miguel G. Cerqueda, Vice President, Operations; Clementina L. Pablo, Resident Manager; Annette Africano, Asst P. R. Manager.

Skyline Restaurant at the World Trade Center: Buendia Avenue at CCP (Cultural Center of the Philippines), Pasay City, Metro Manila.
Tel.: (632) 551-7524/551-5244;
Fax.: (632) 551-5244.
Lynn Raquel Santos-Sunico, President and General Manager; Offie Datoc Evangelista; Food and Beverage Consultant and Stylist.

Villa Escudero Plantations and Resort: San Pablo City. Manila office – 1059 Estrada St, Malate 1004, Manila.
Tel.: (632)521-0830/523-2944;
Fax.: (632) 521-8698.
Conrado A. Escudero, President and Executive Chef; Mari A. Escudero, Food and Beverage Manager; Lito Dalangin, Chef; Lil Capunatan; Willy de Rosalis.

The Westin Philippine Plaza: CCP Complex, Roxas Boulevard, Pasay City 1300, Metro Manila.
Tel.: (632) 551-5555;
Fax.: (632) 551-5610.
John F. Swaney, General Manager; Sandra Garcia, Director of Sales and Marketing; Tim Steckbeck, Director of Food and Beverages; Chef Vincent Yap; Chef Thomas Wee; Michelle Marcelo, Treasure Island Manager; Elizabeth Timbol, Public Relations Officer; Daisy Carandang, Public Relations Secretary.

Index